Relaxing Summer Fun Coloring Book

ISBN-13: 978-1535106290
ISBN-10: 1535106298

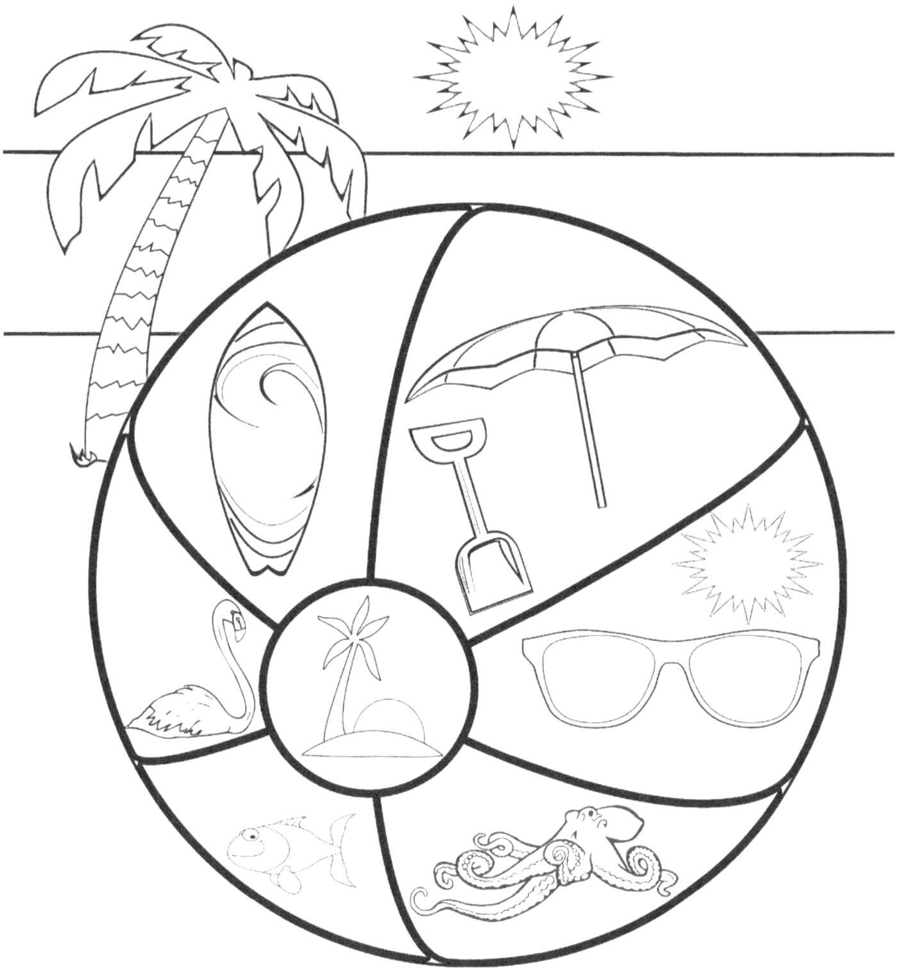

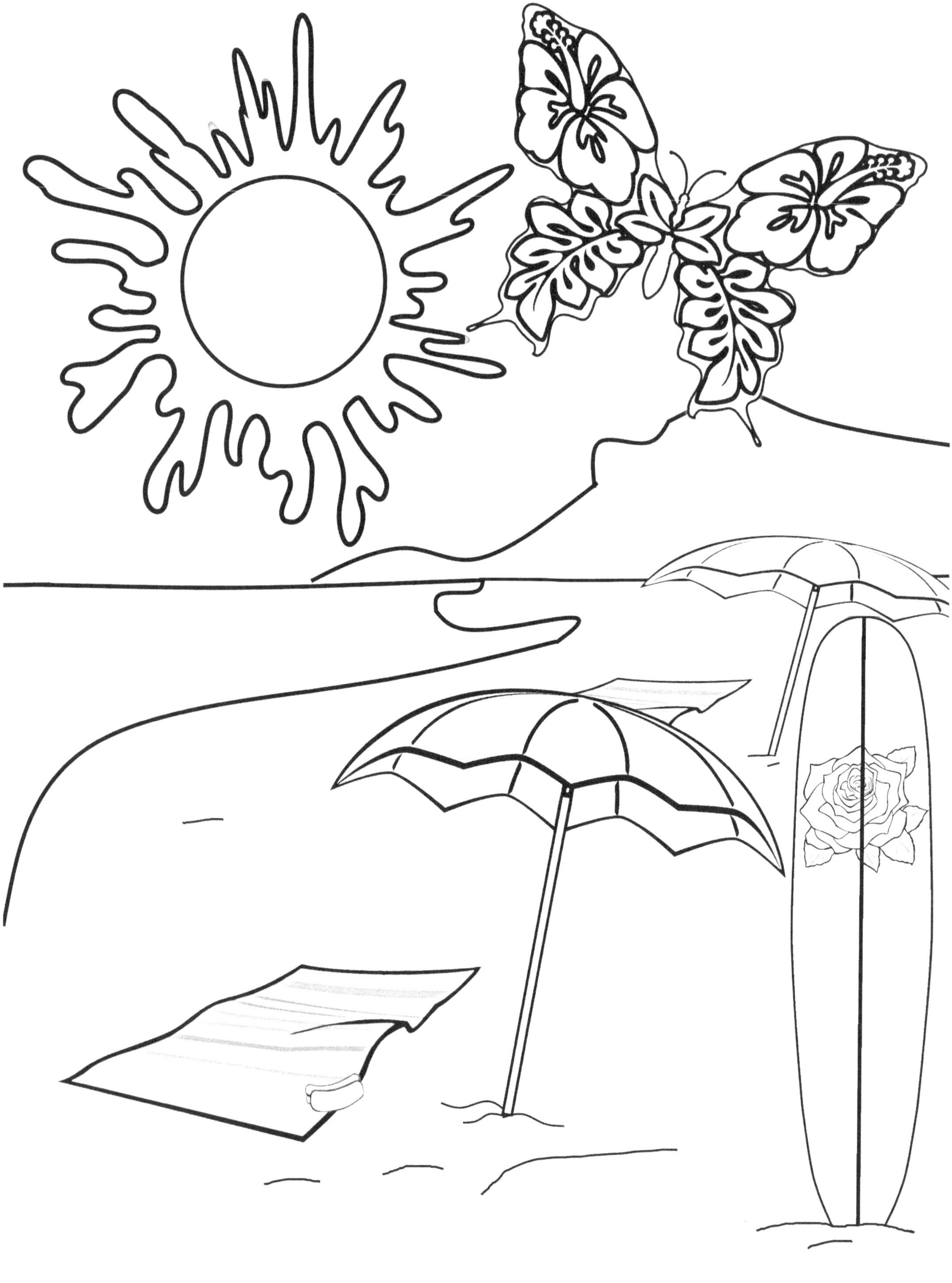

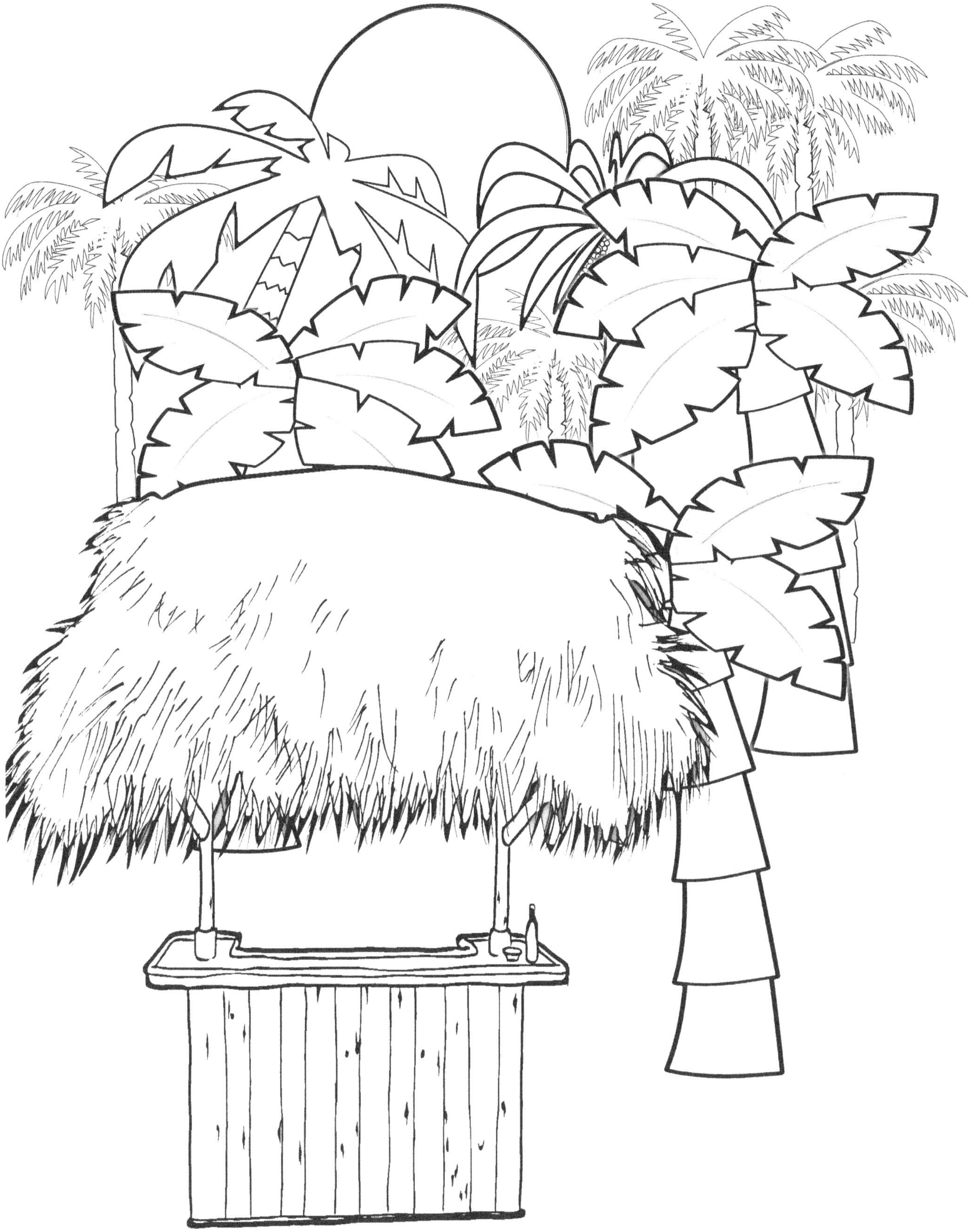

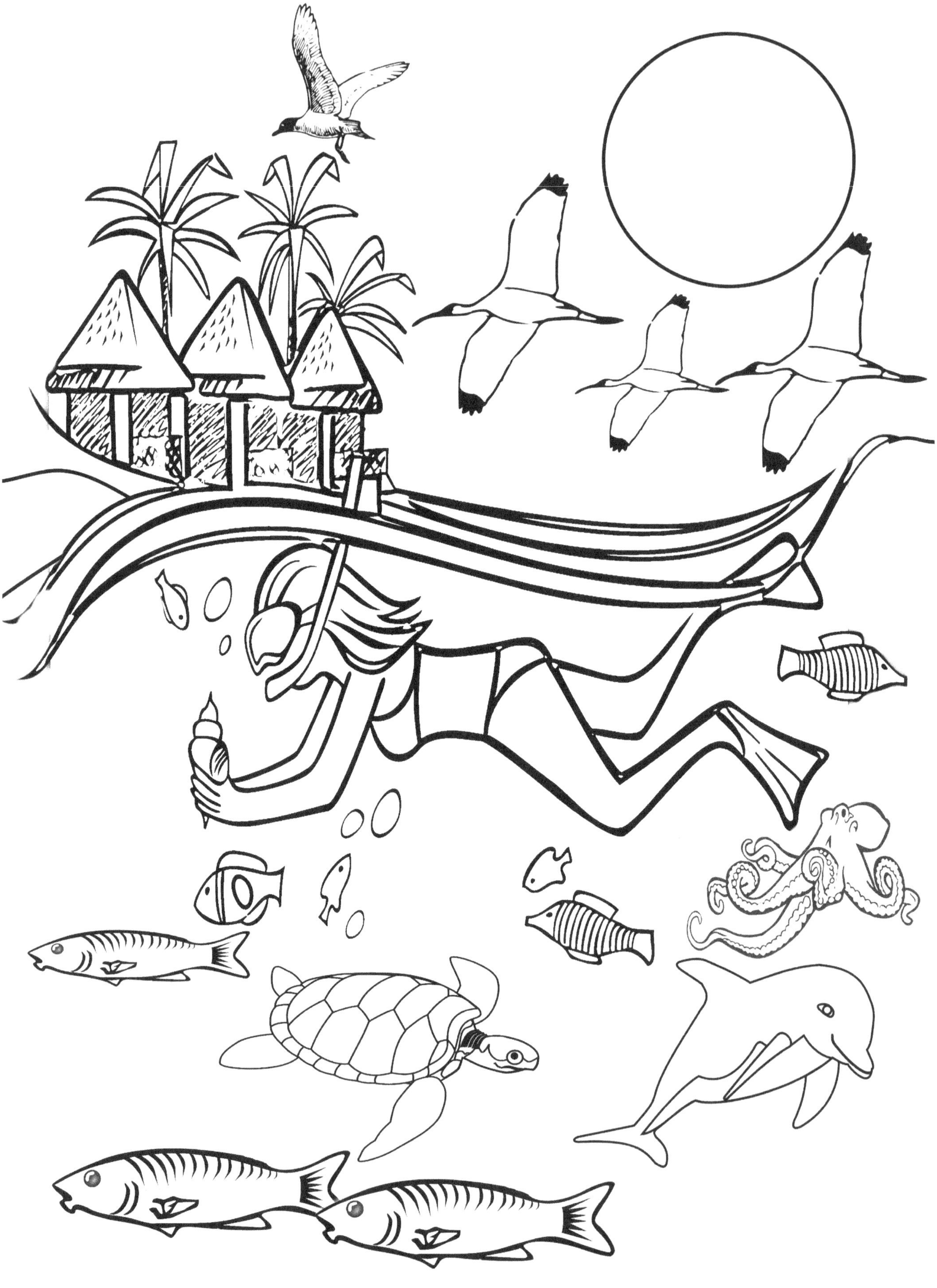

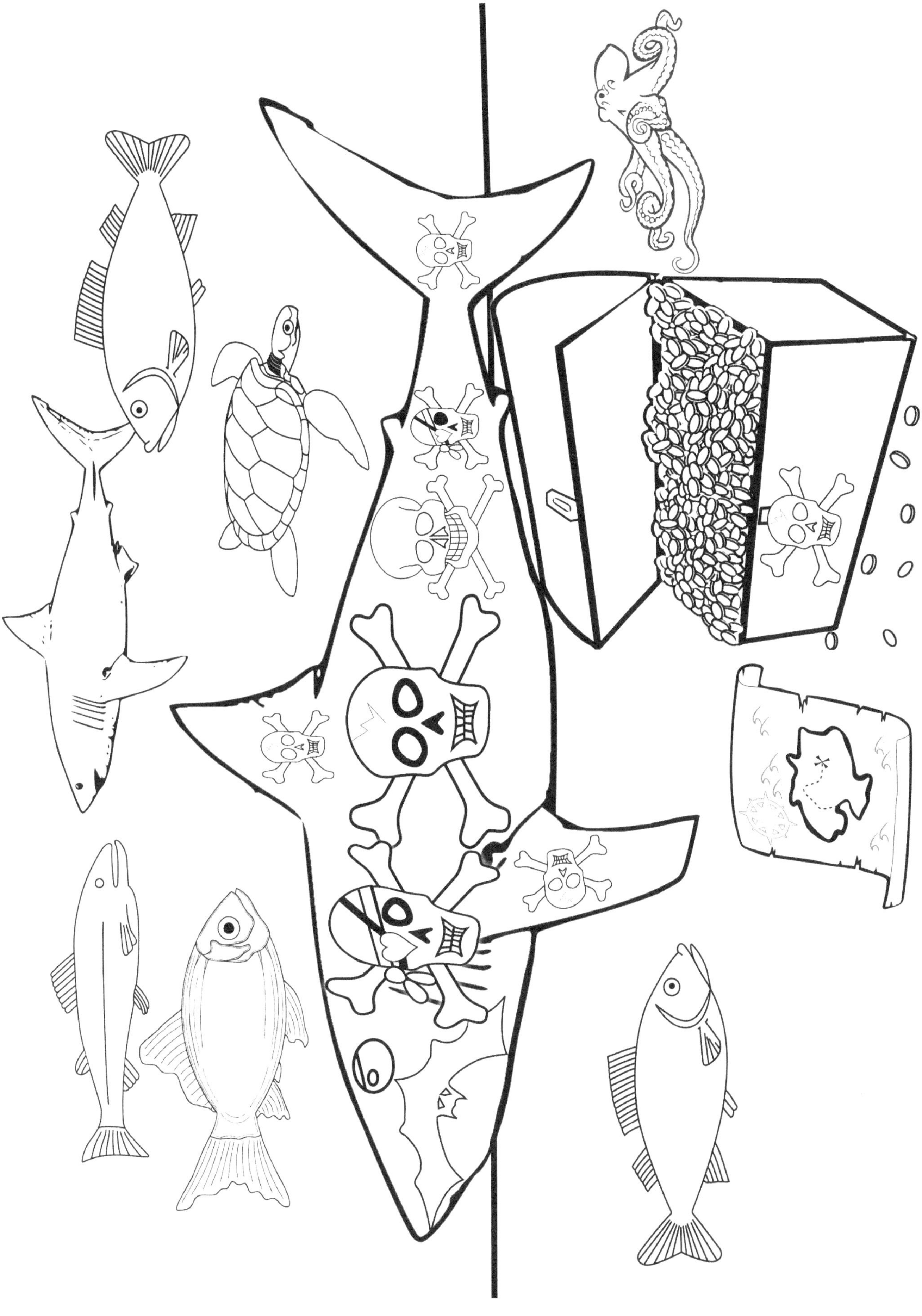

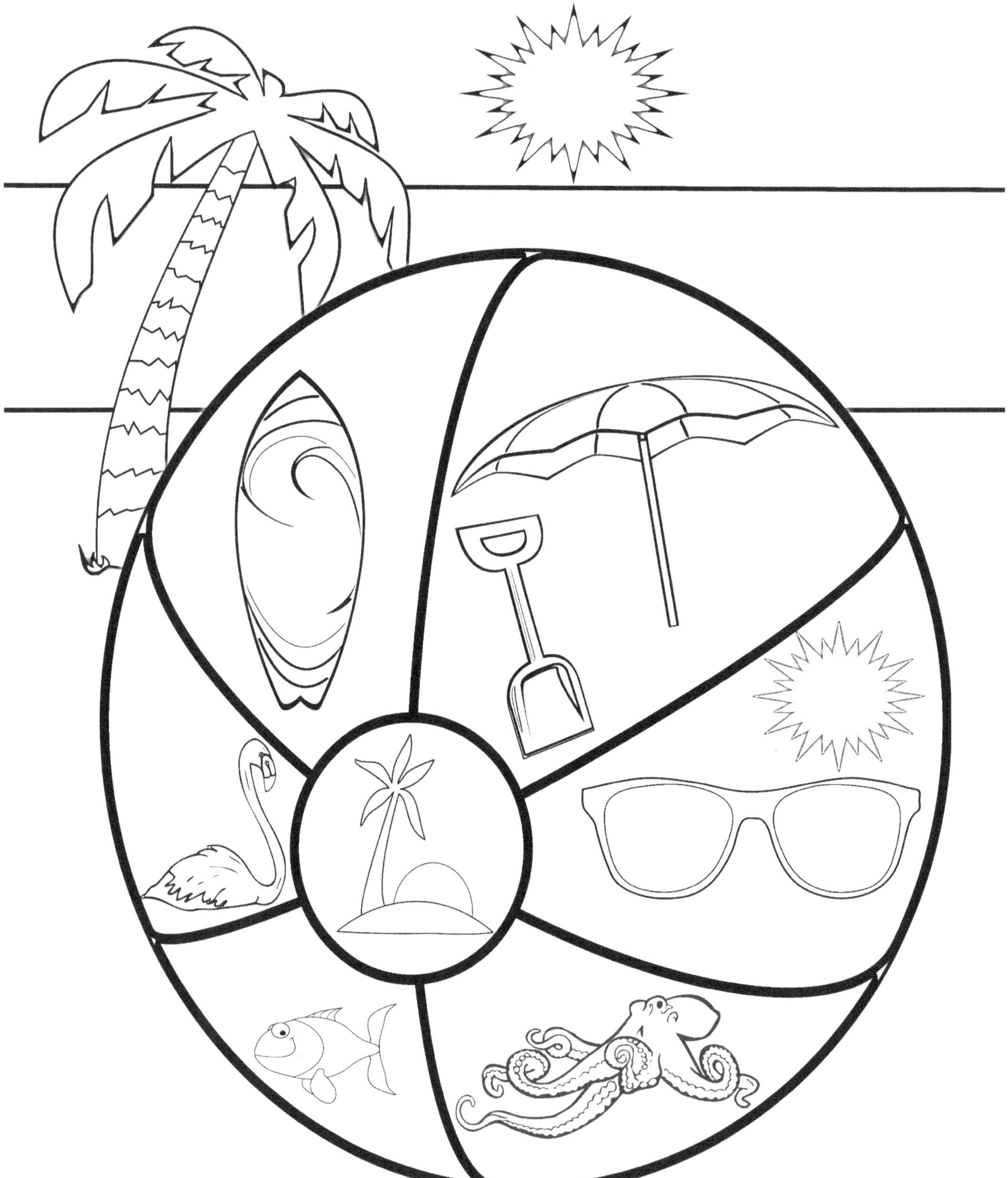

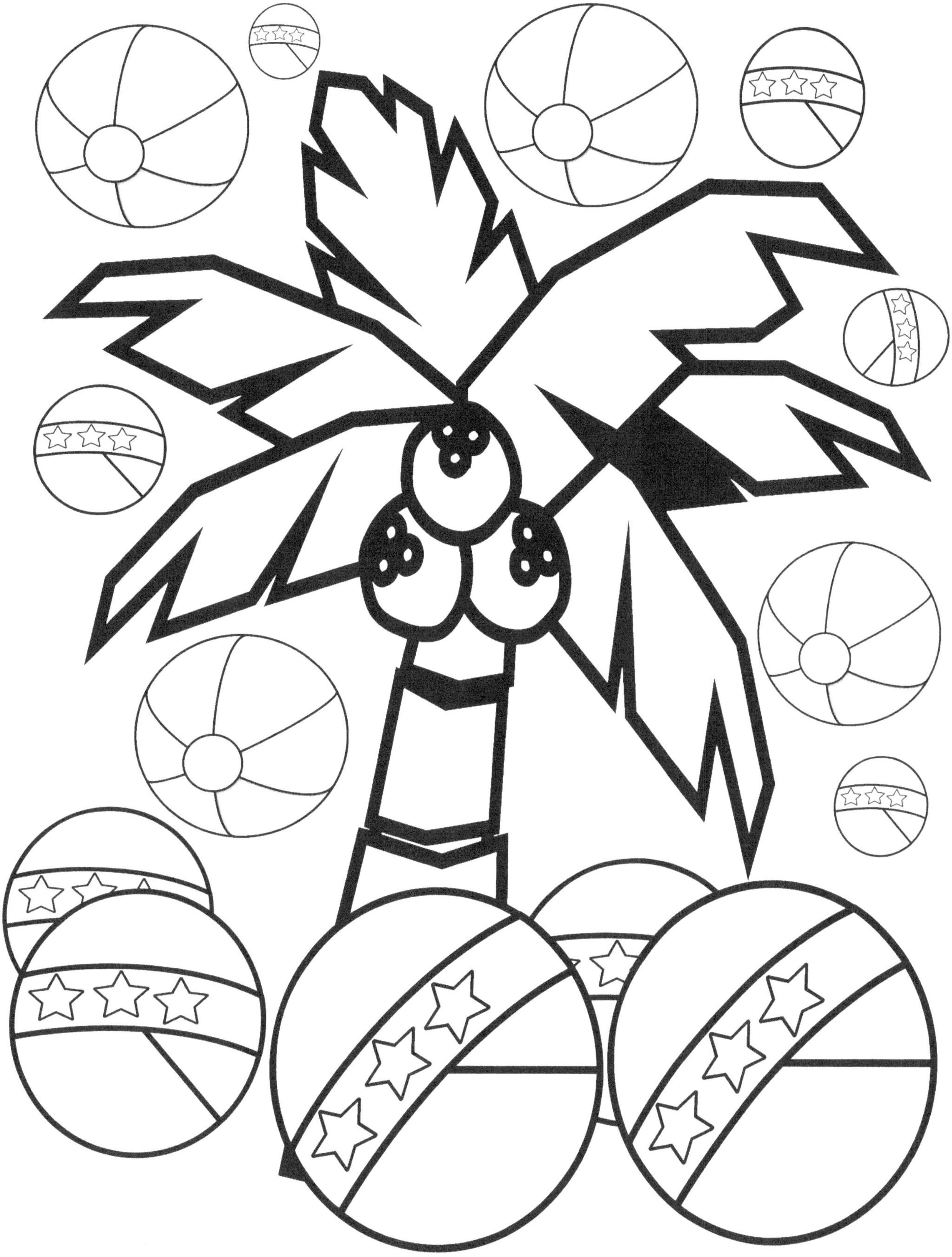

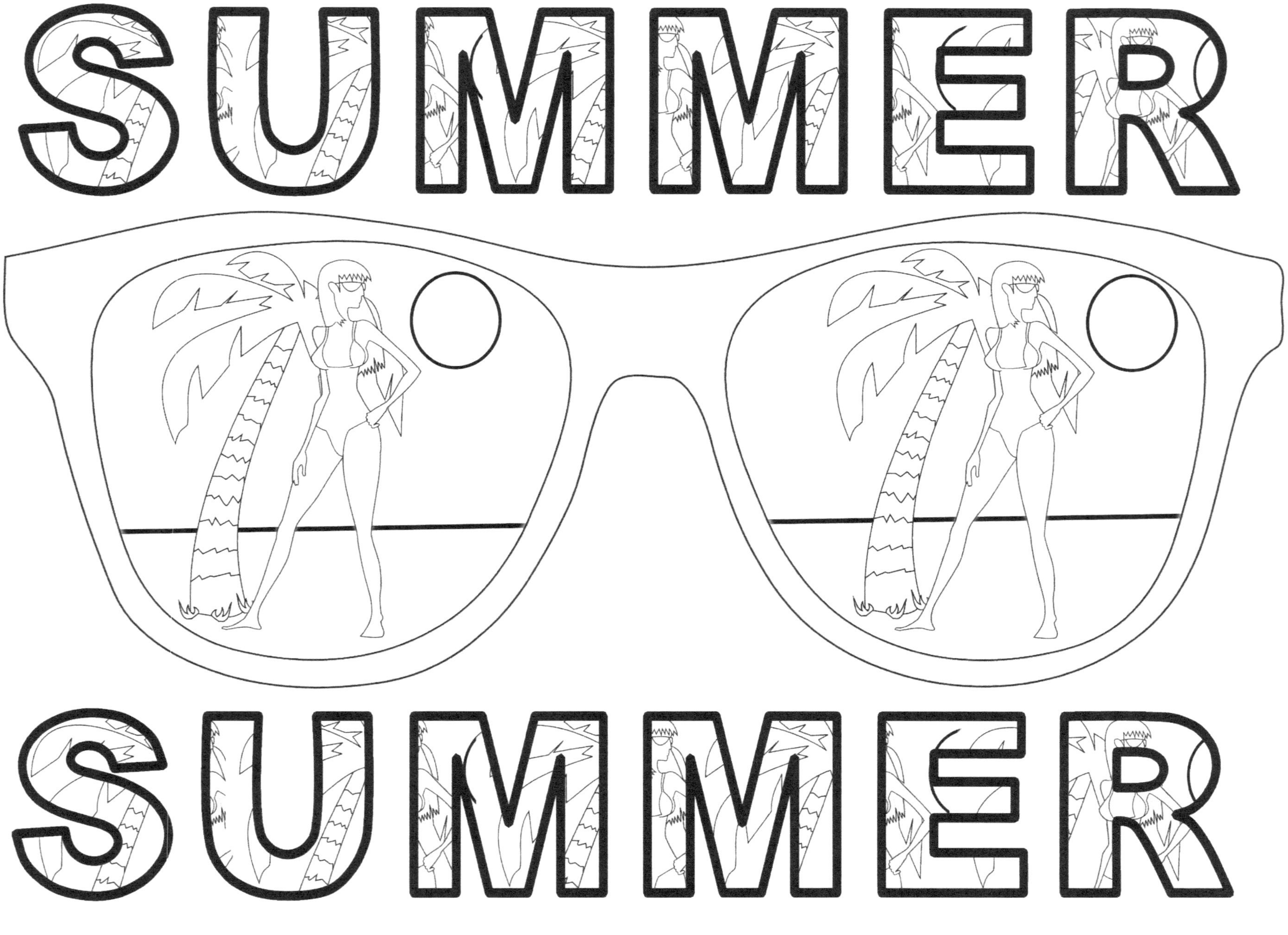
SUMMER
SUMMER

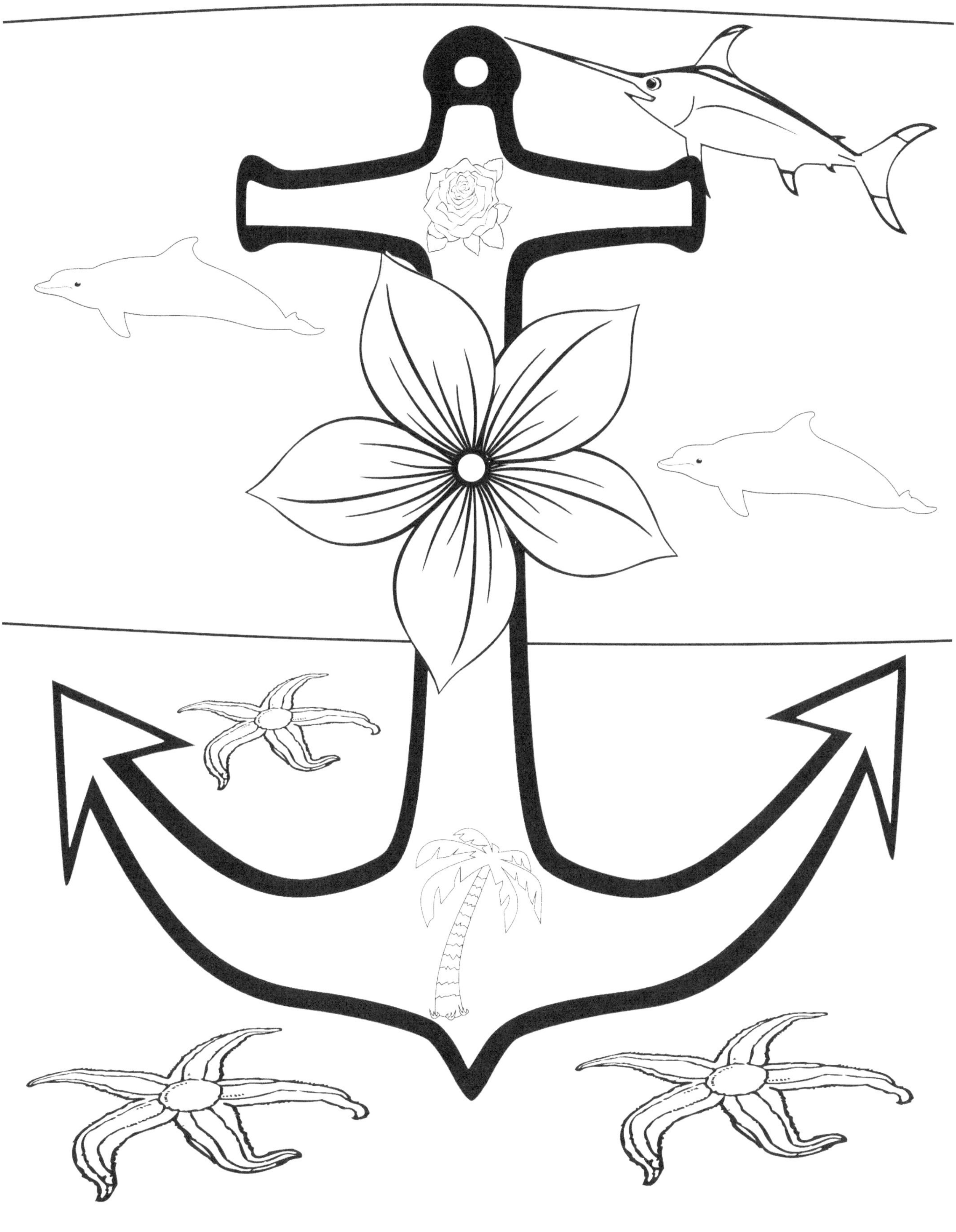

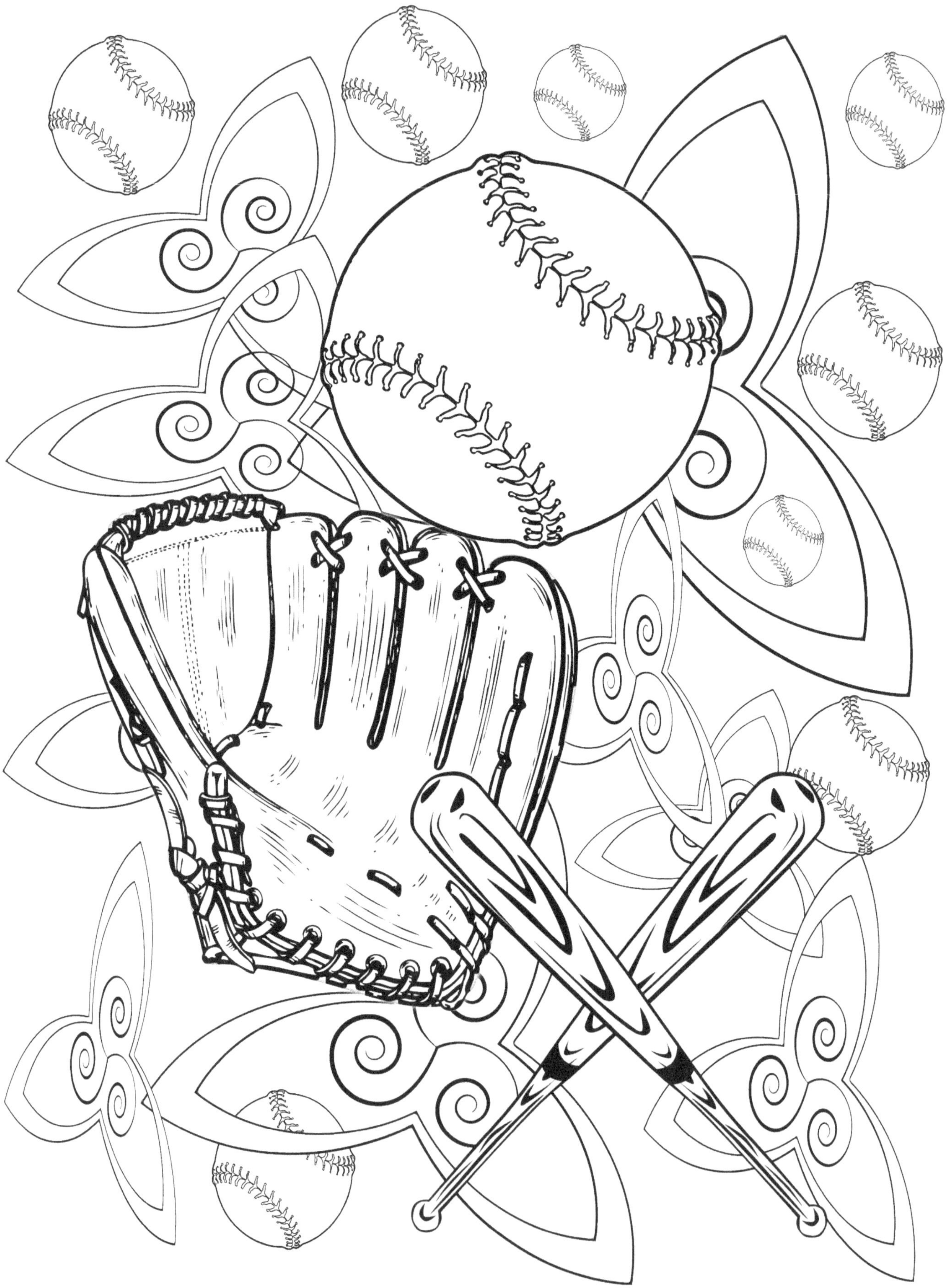

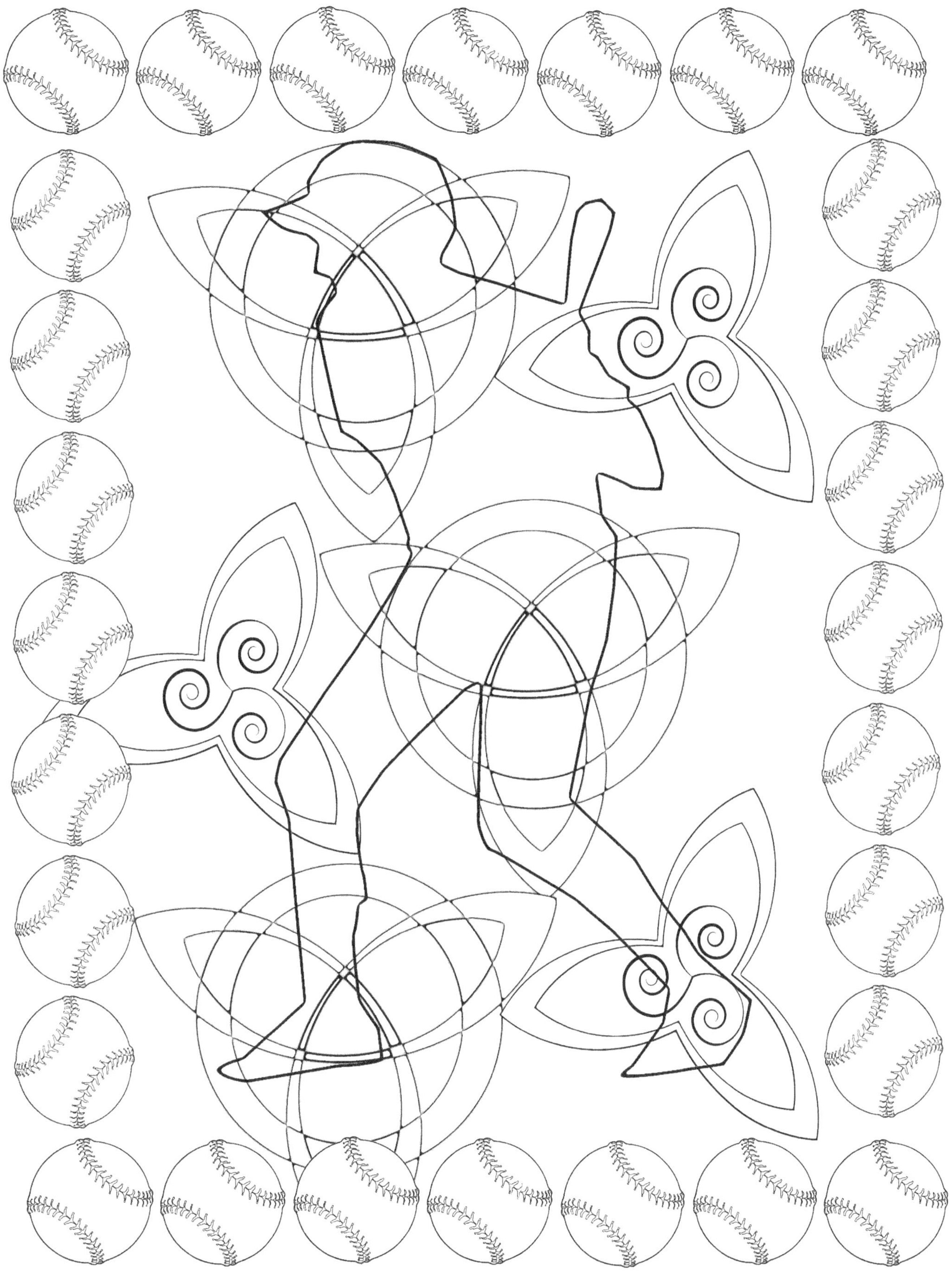

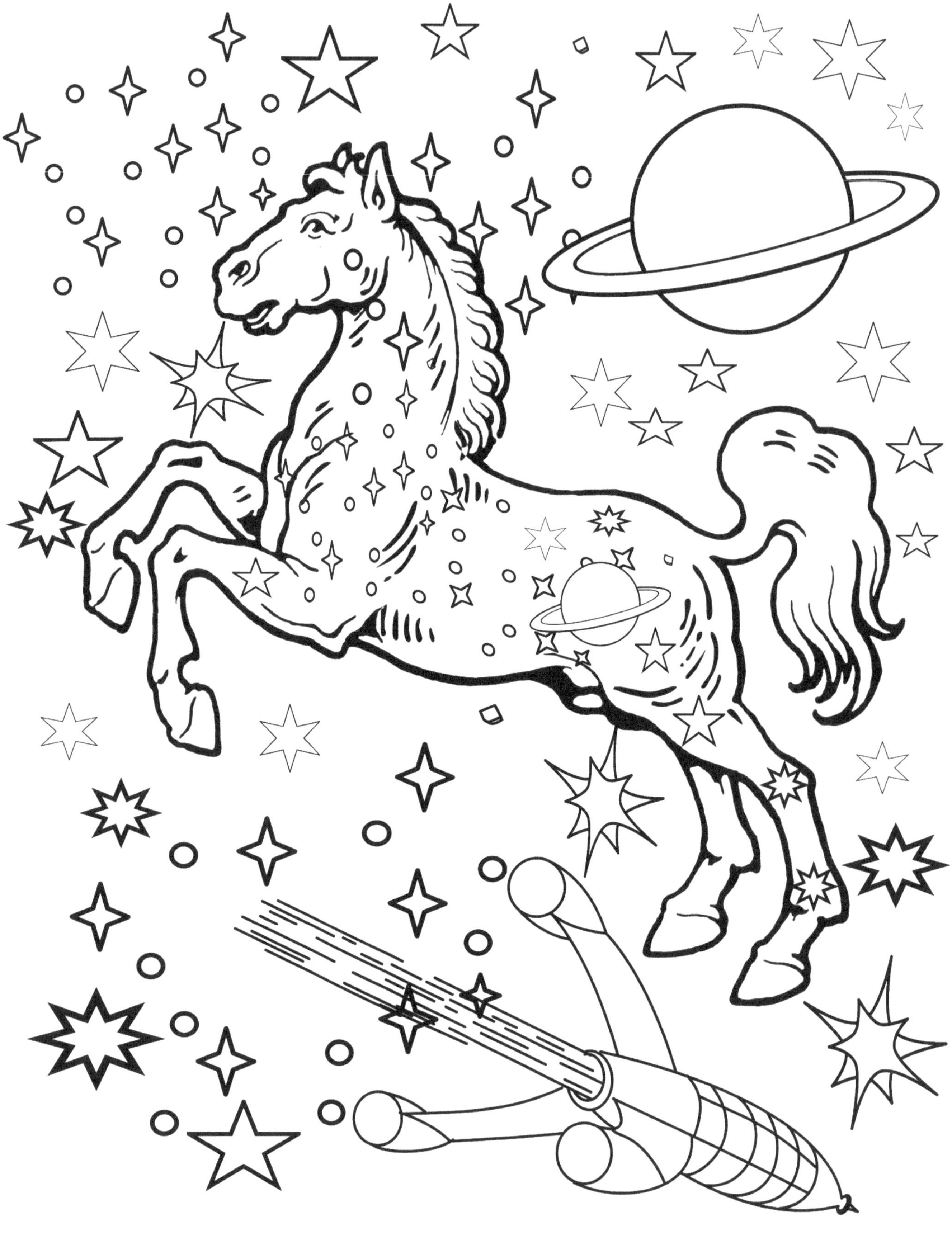

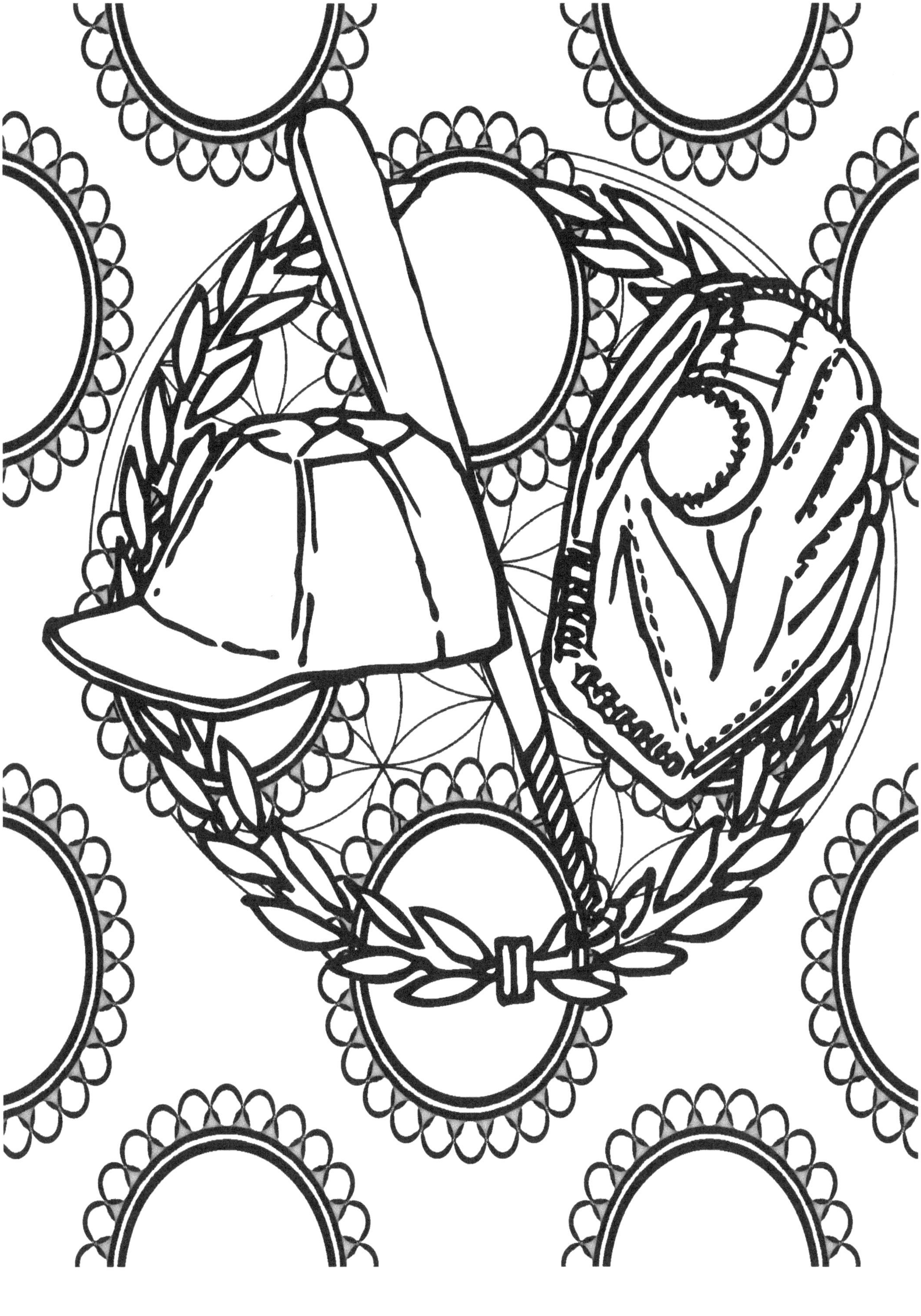

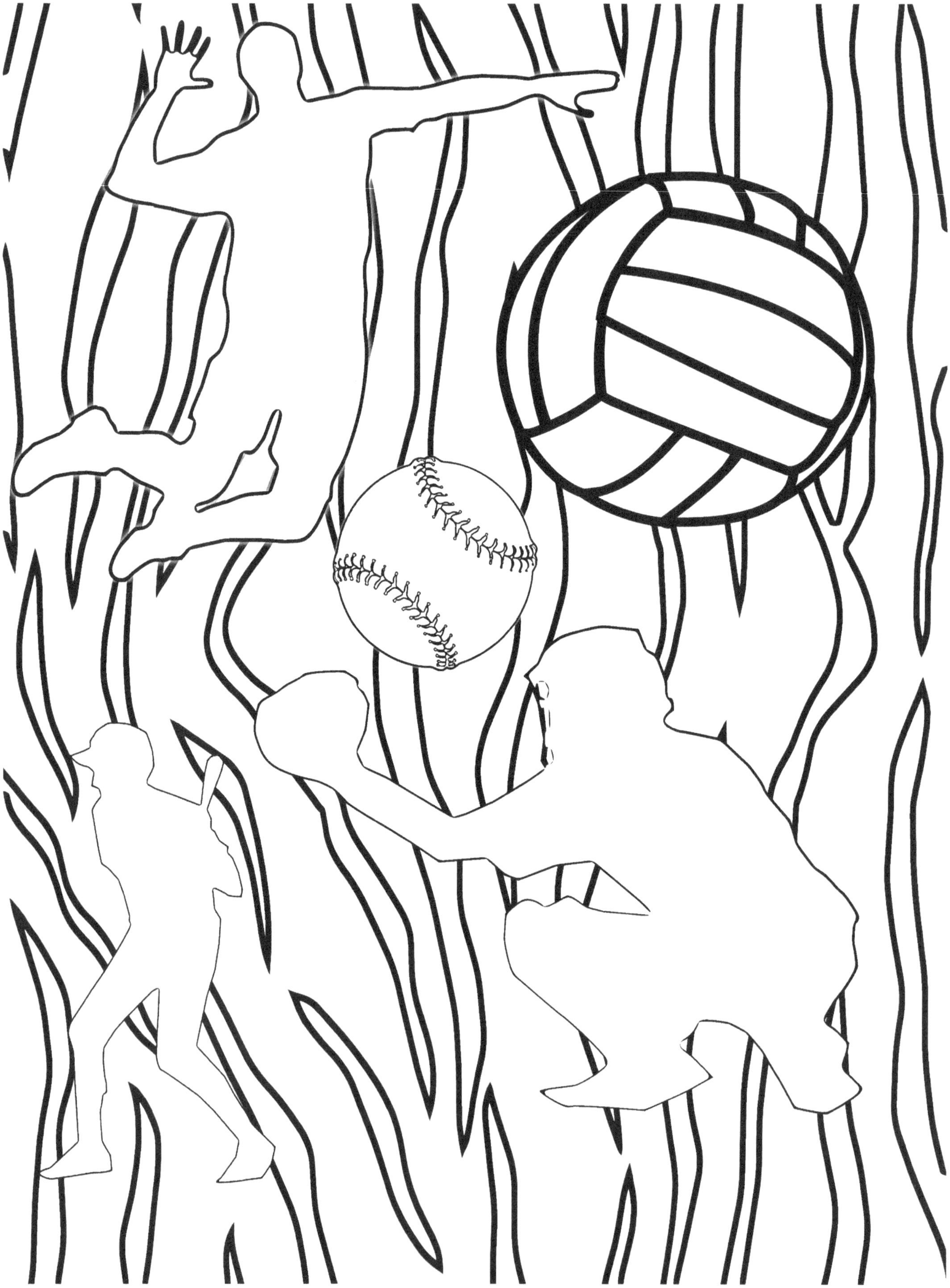

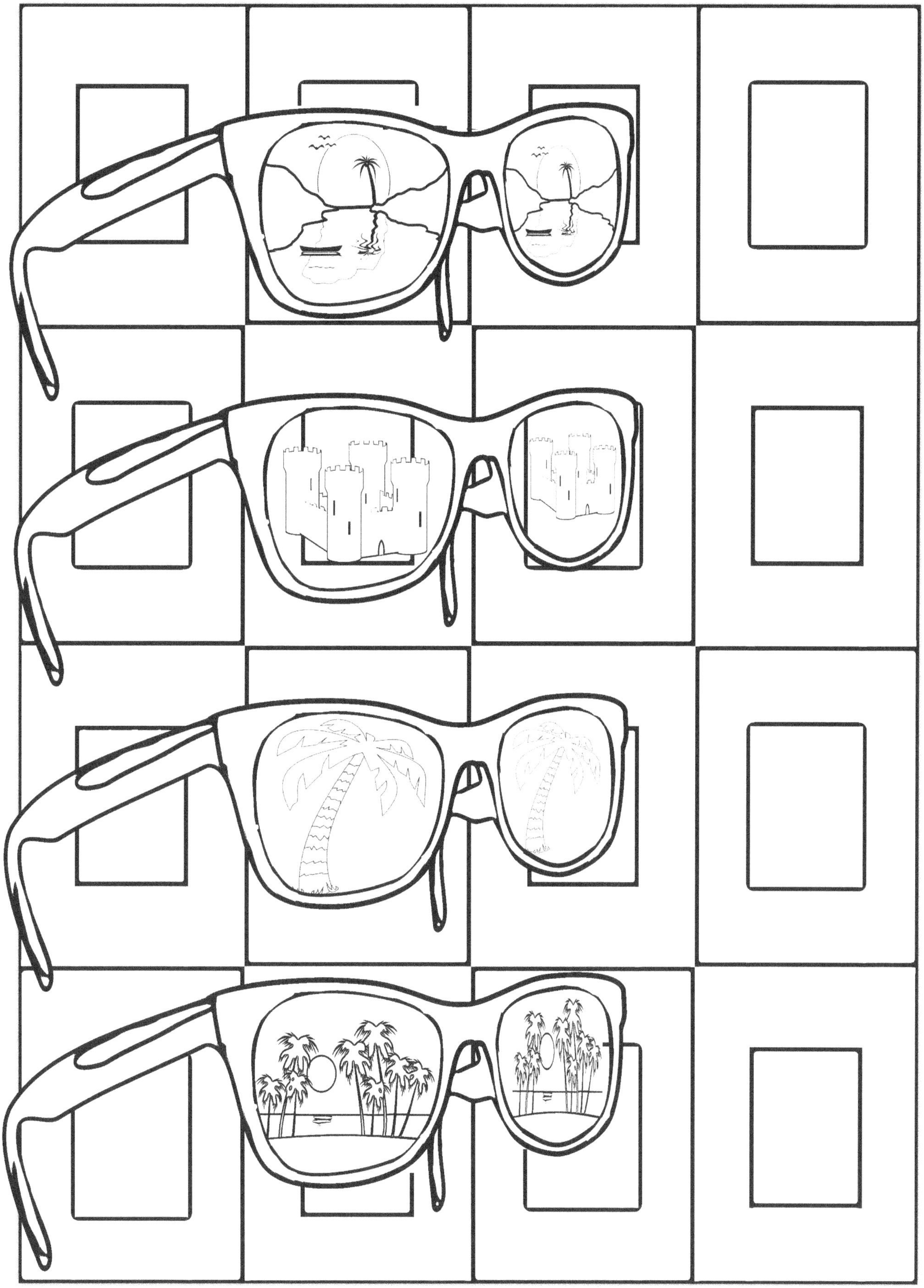

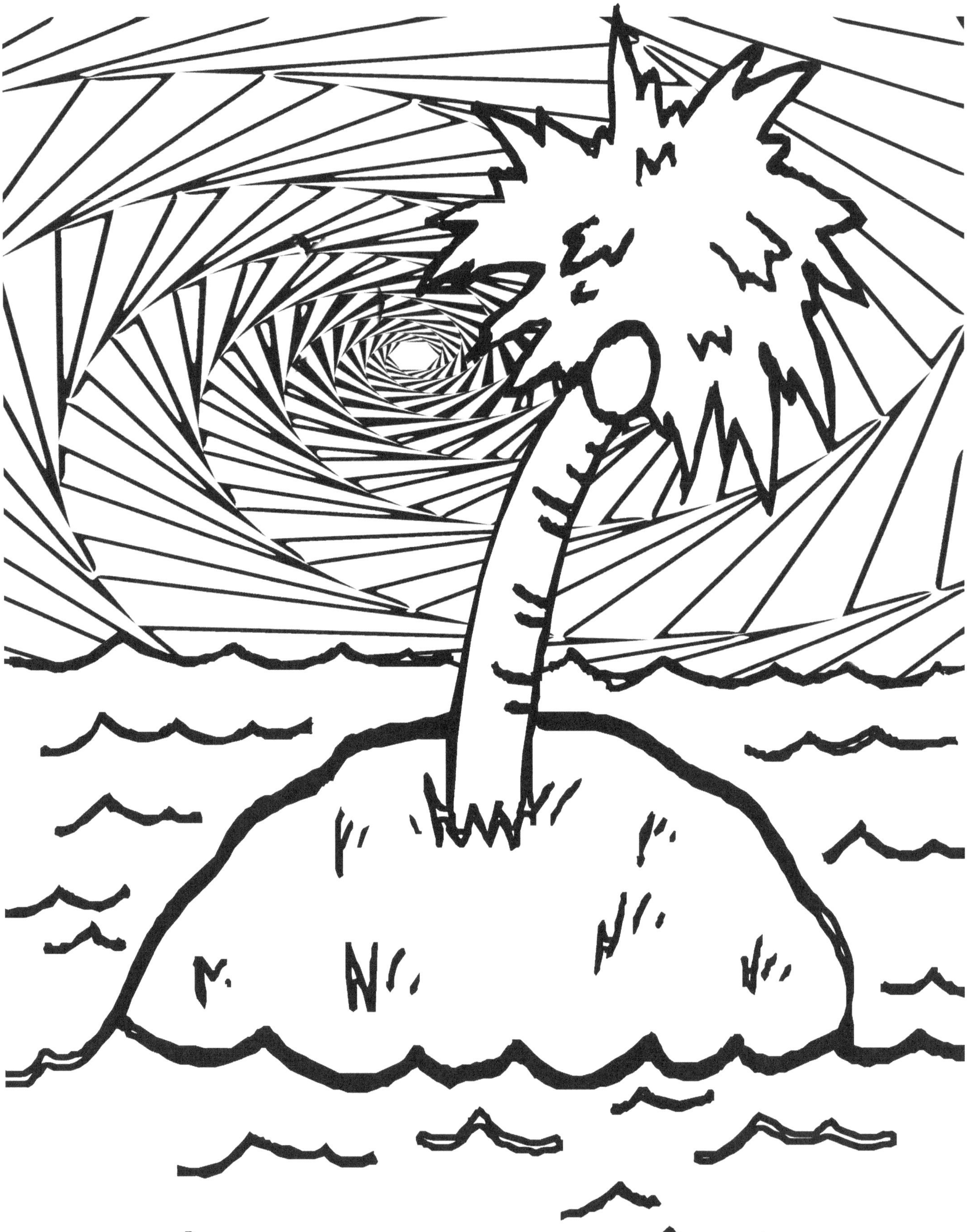

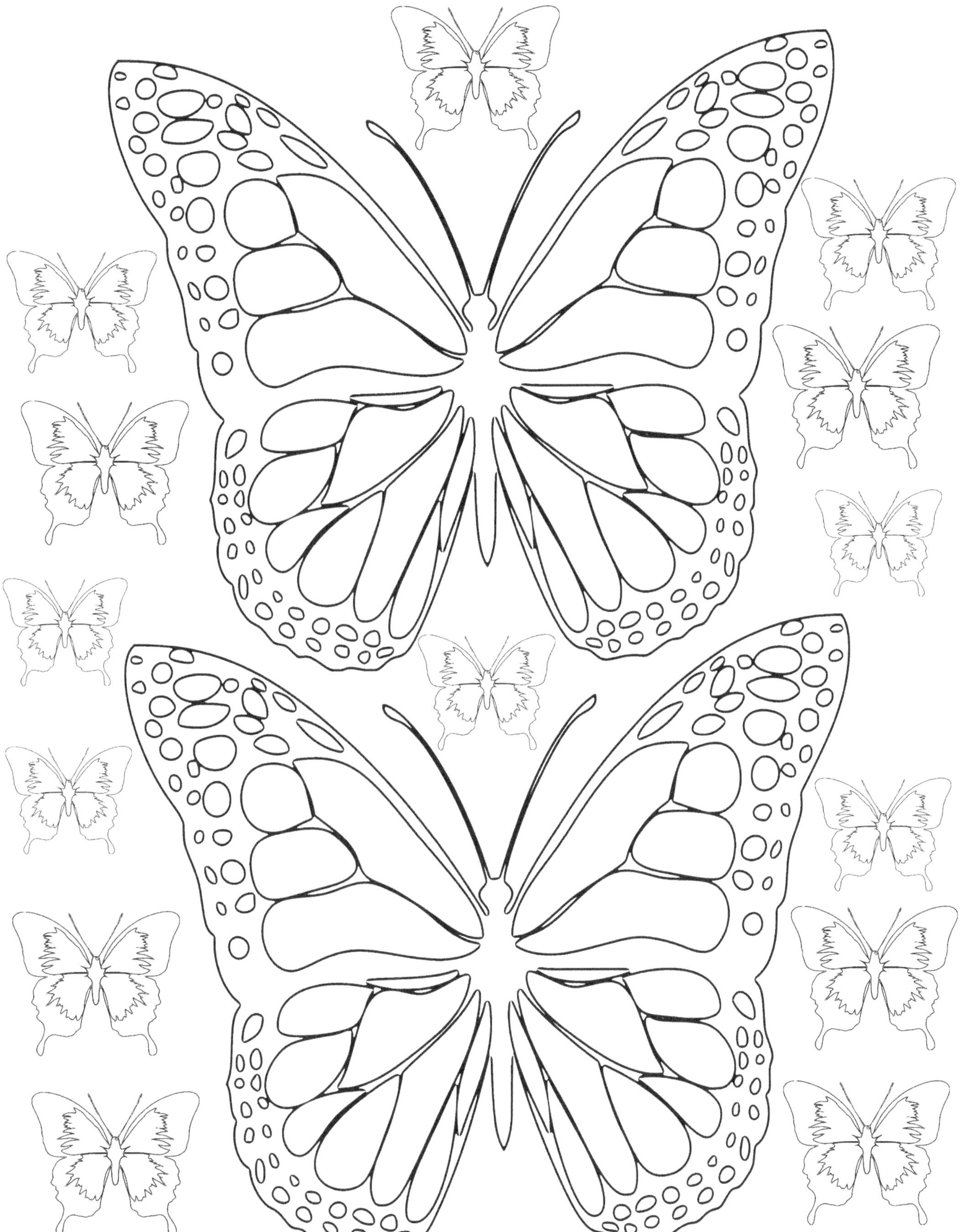

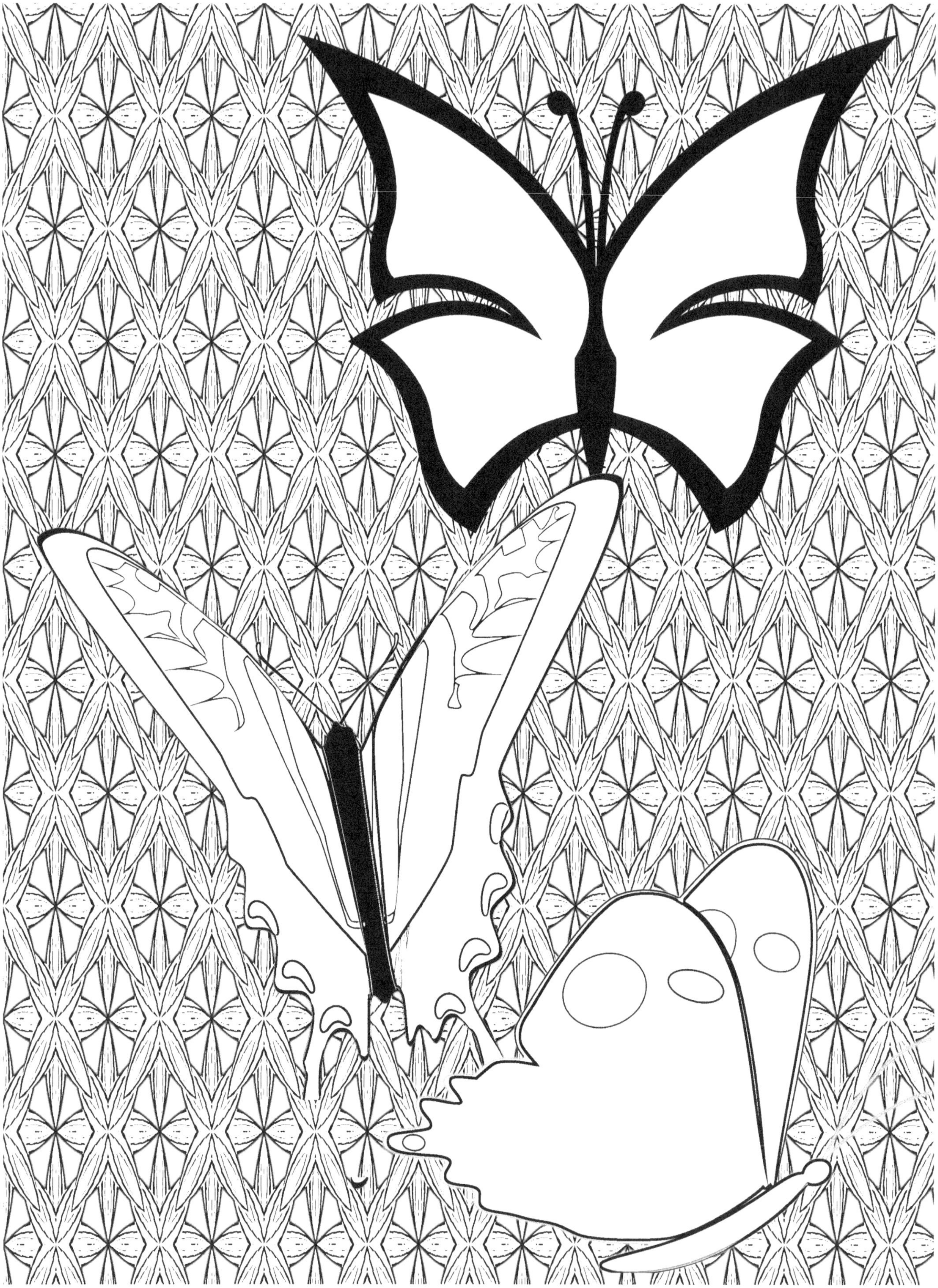

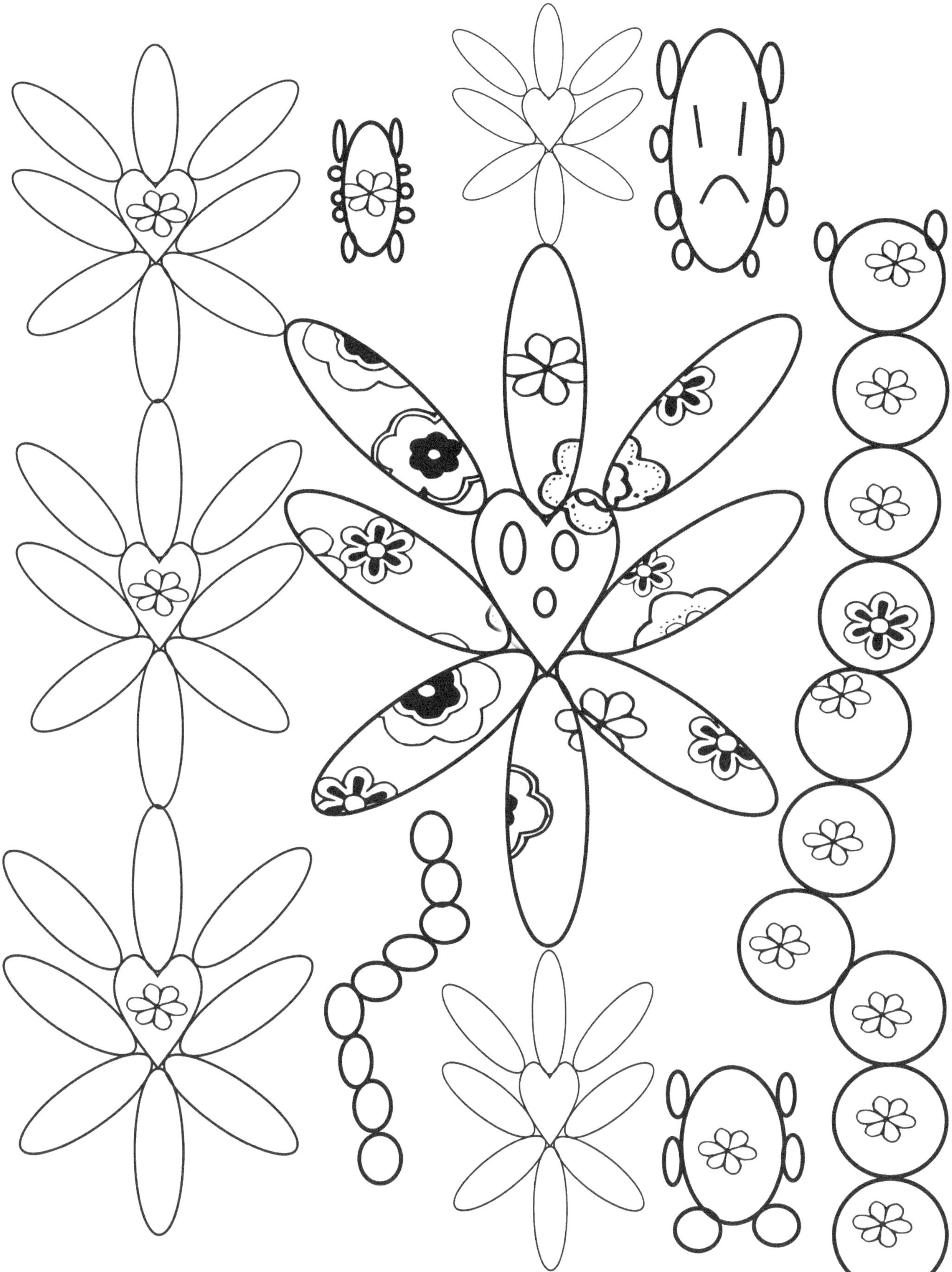

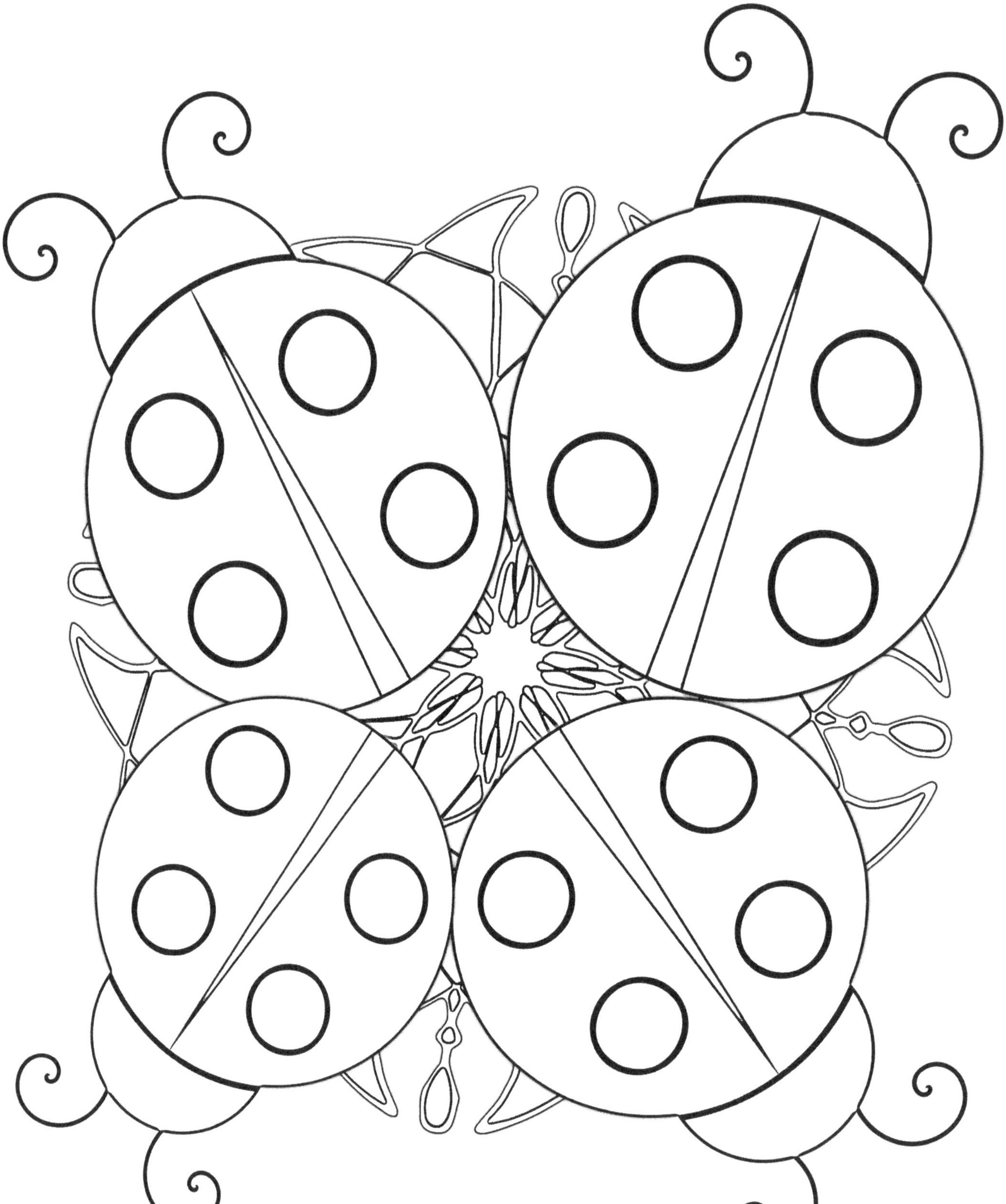

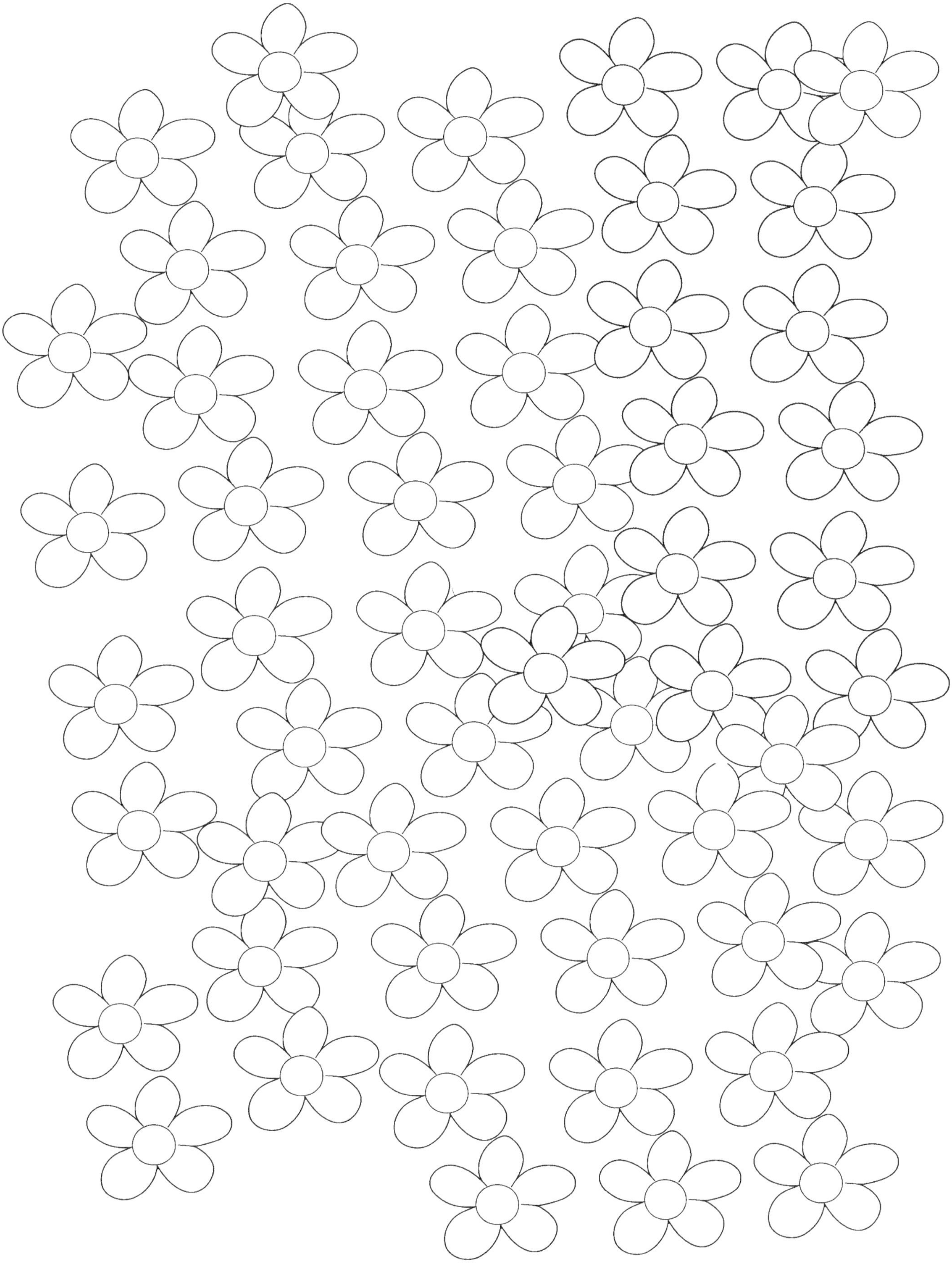

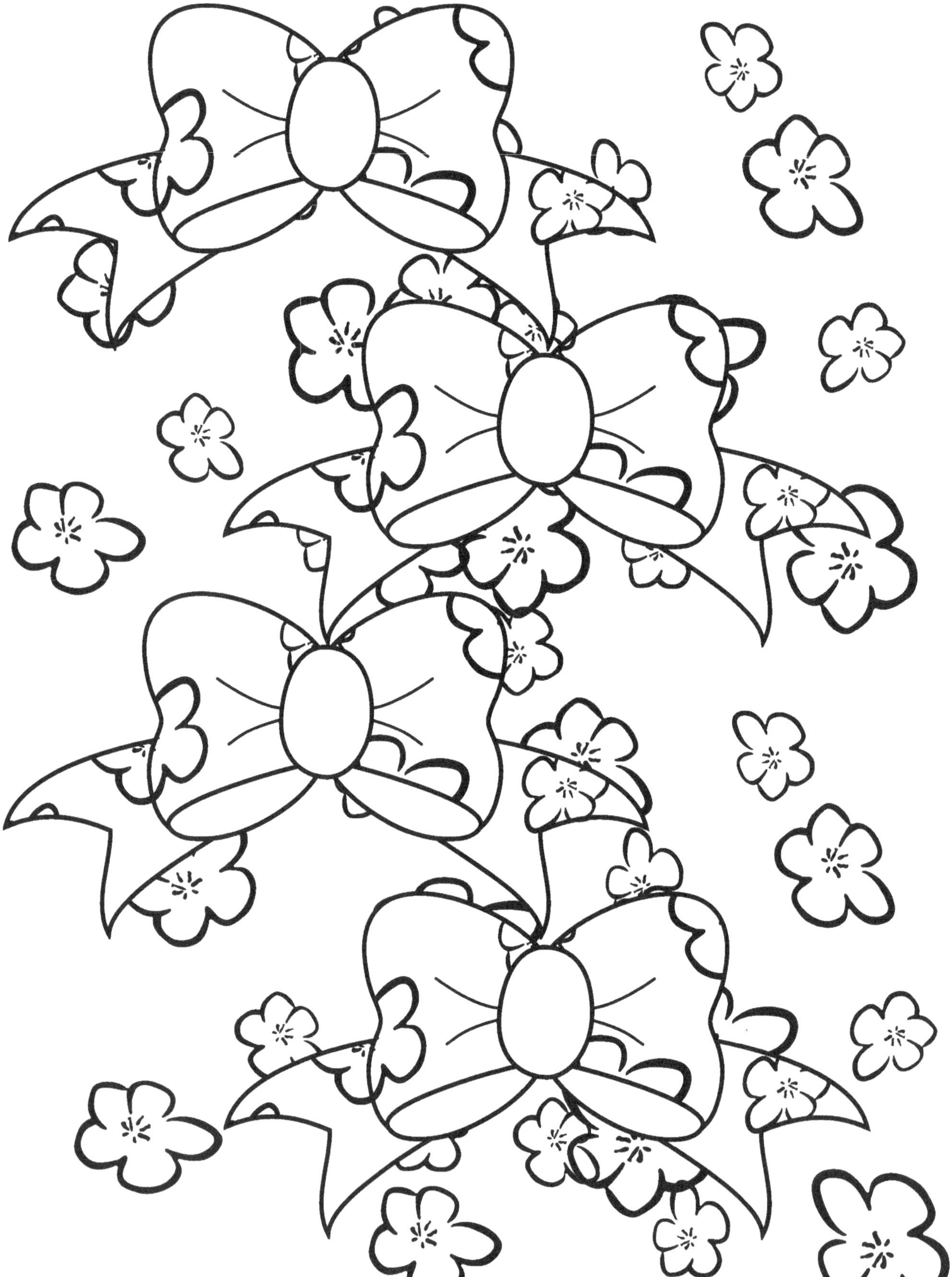

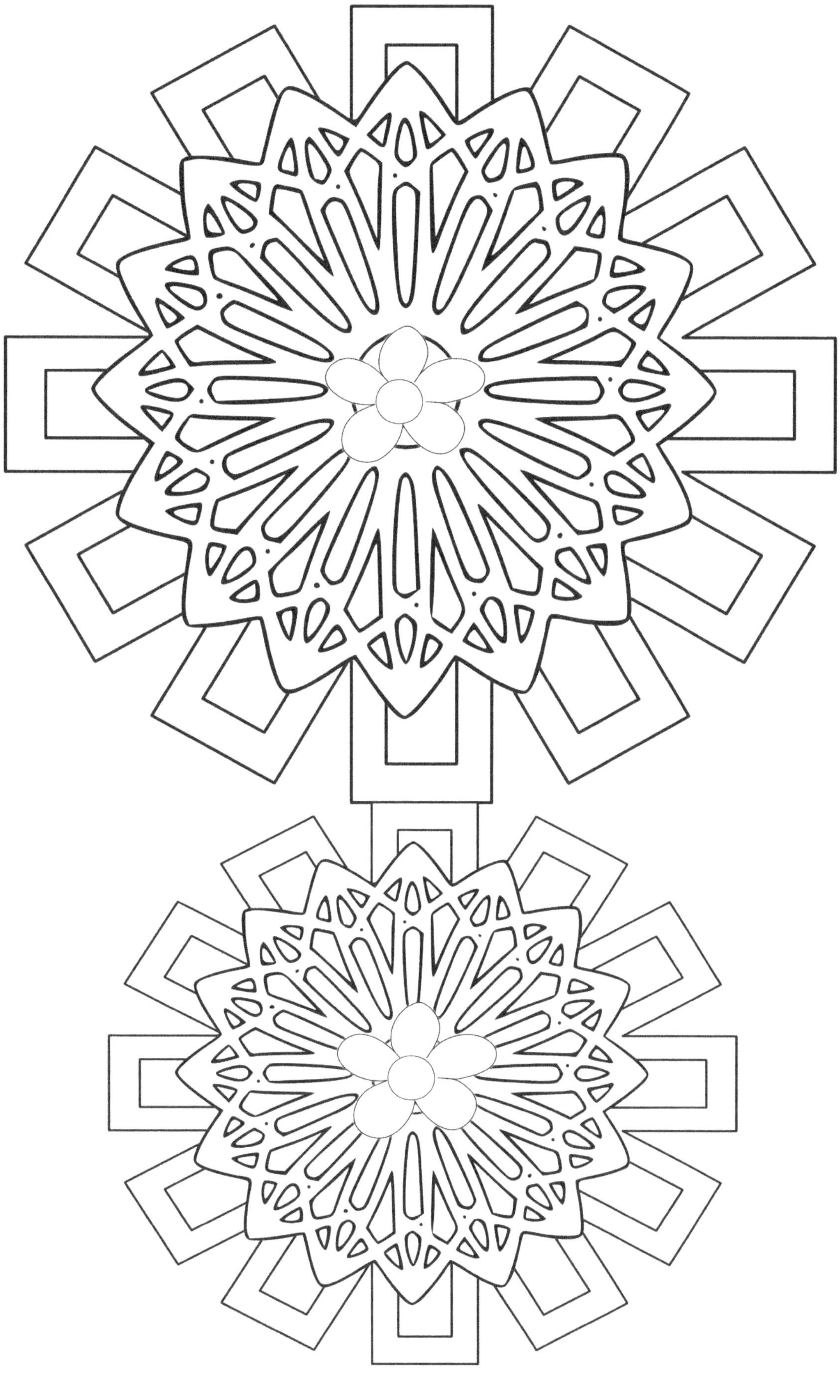

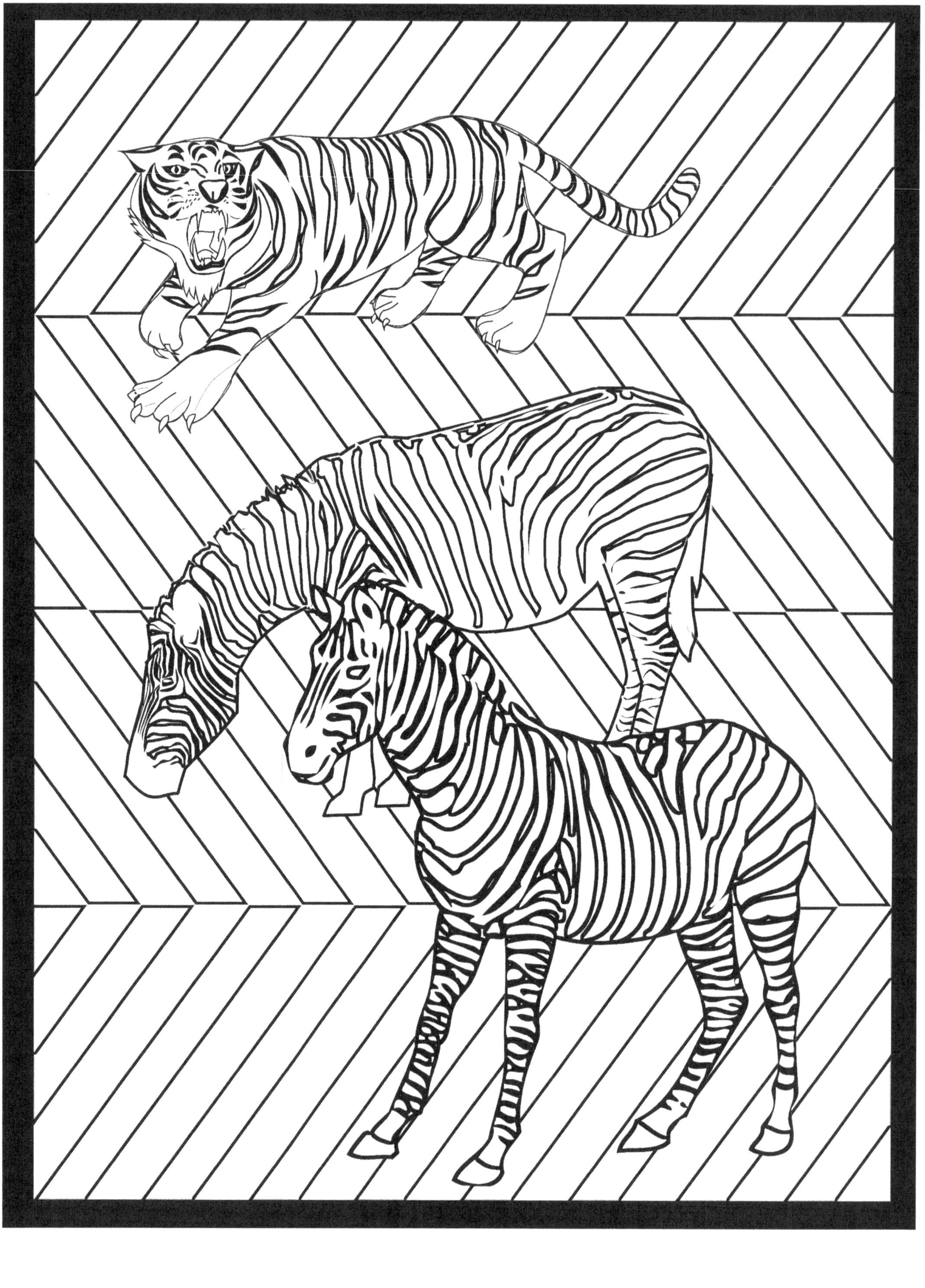

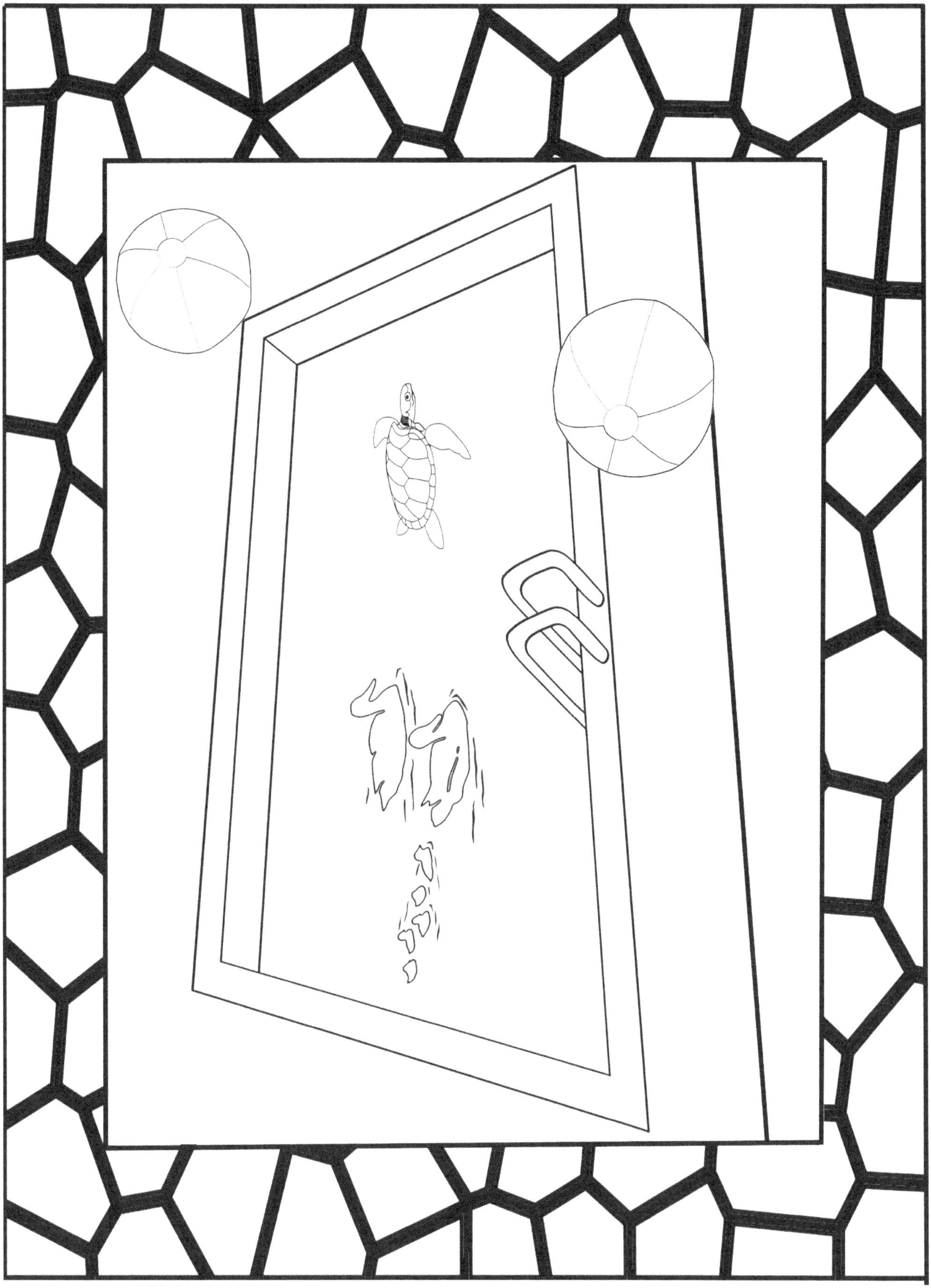

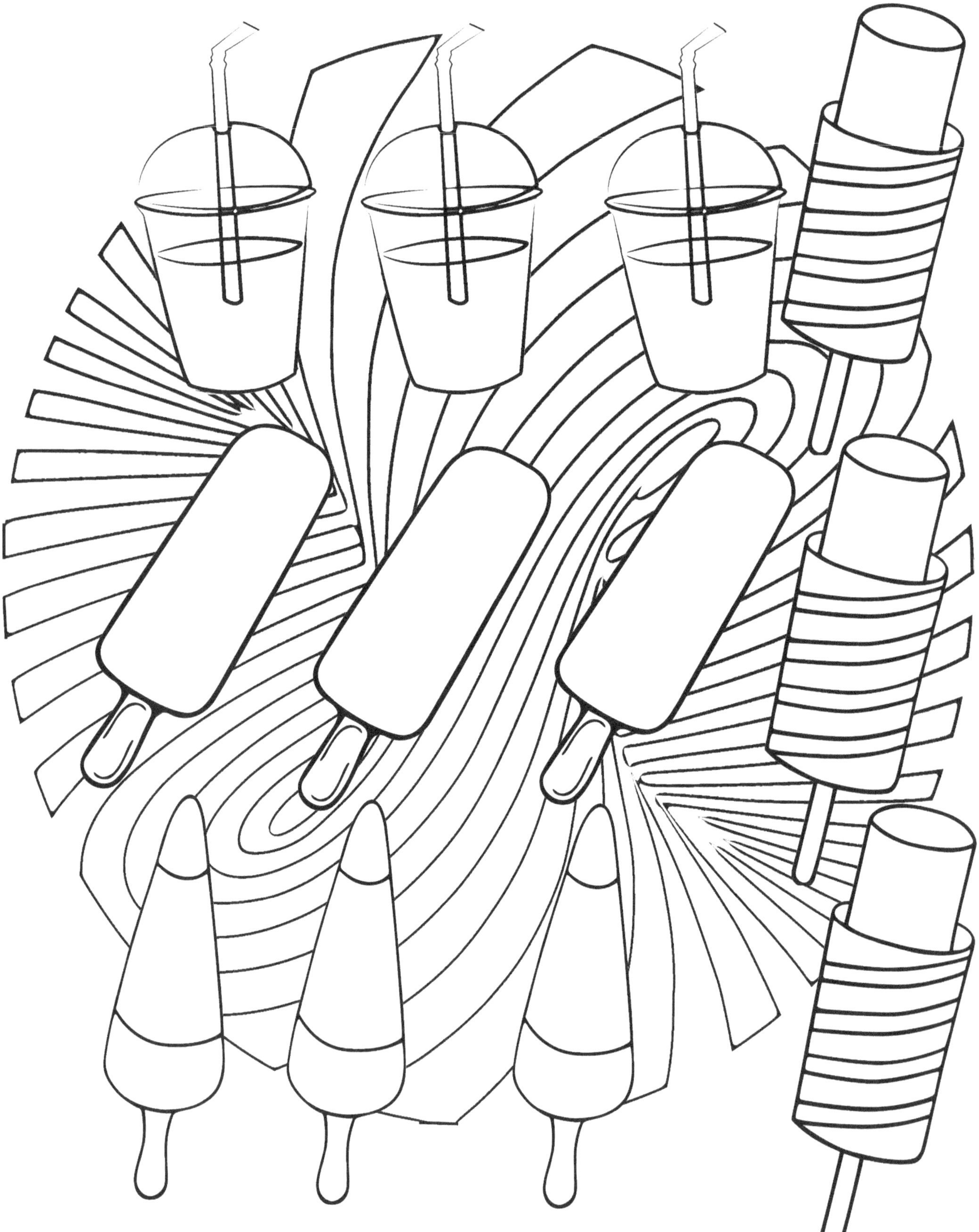

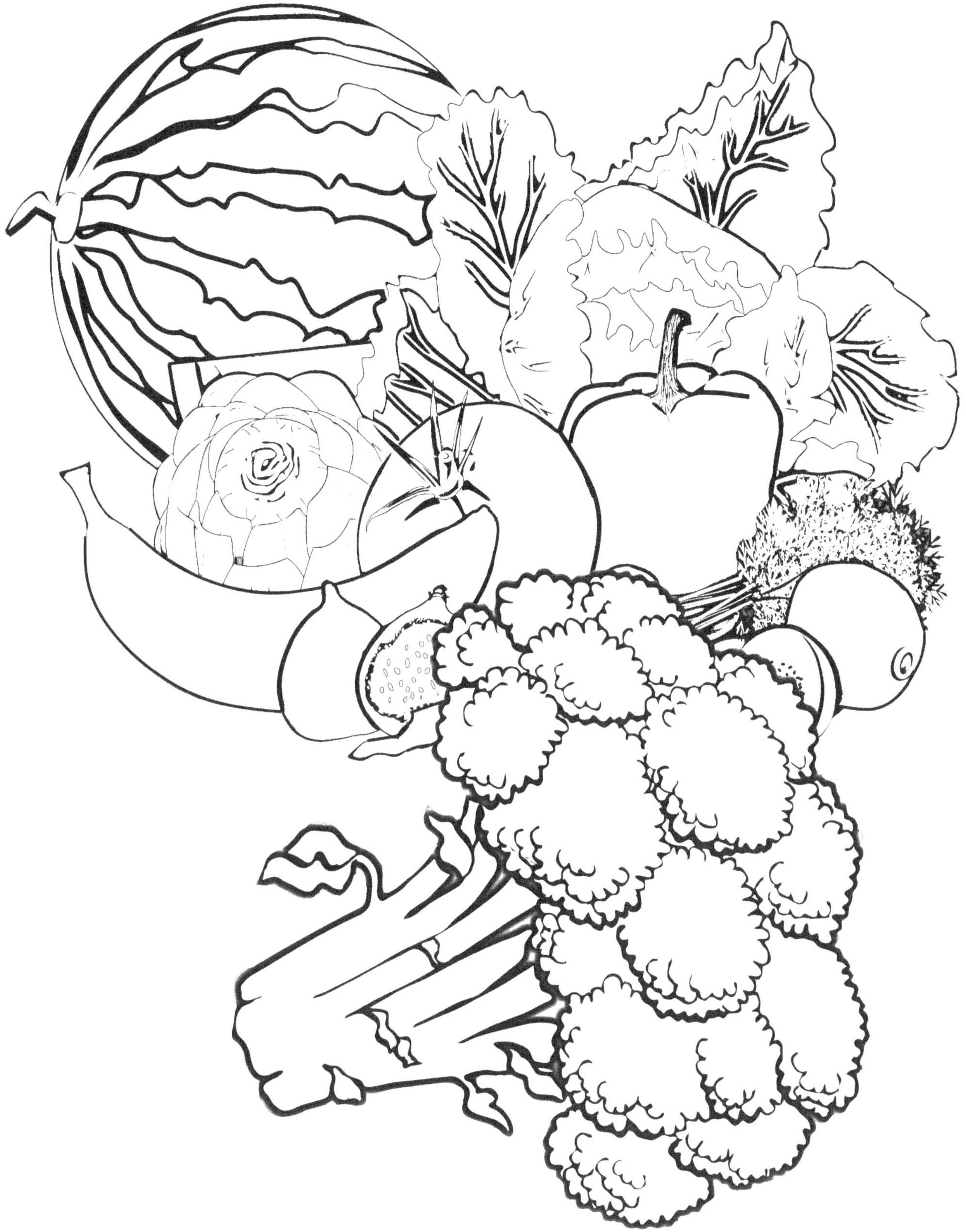

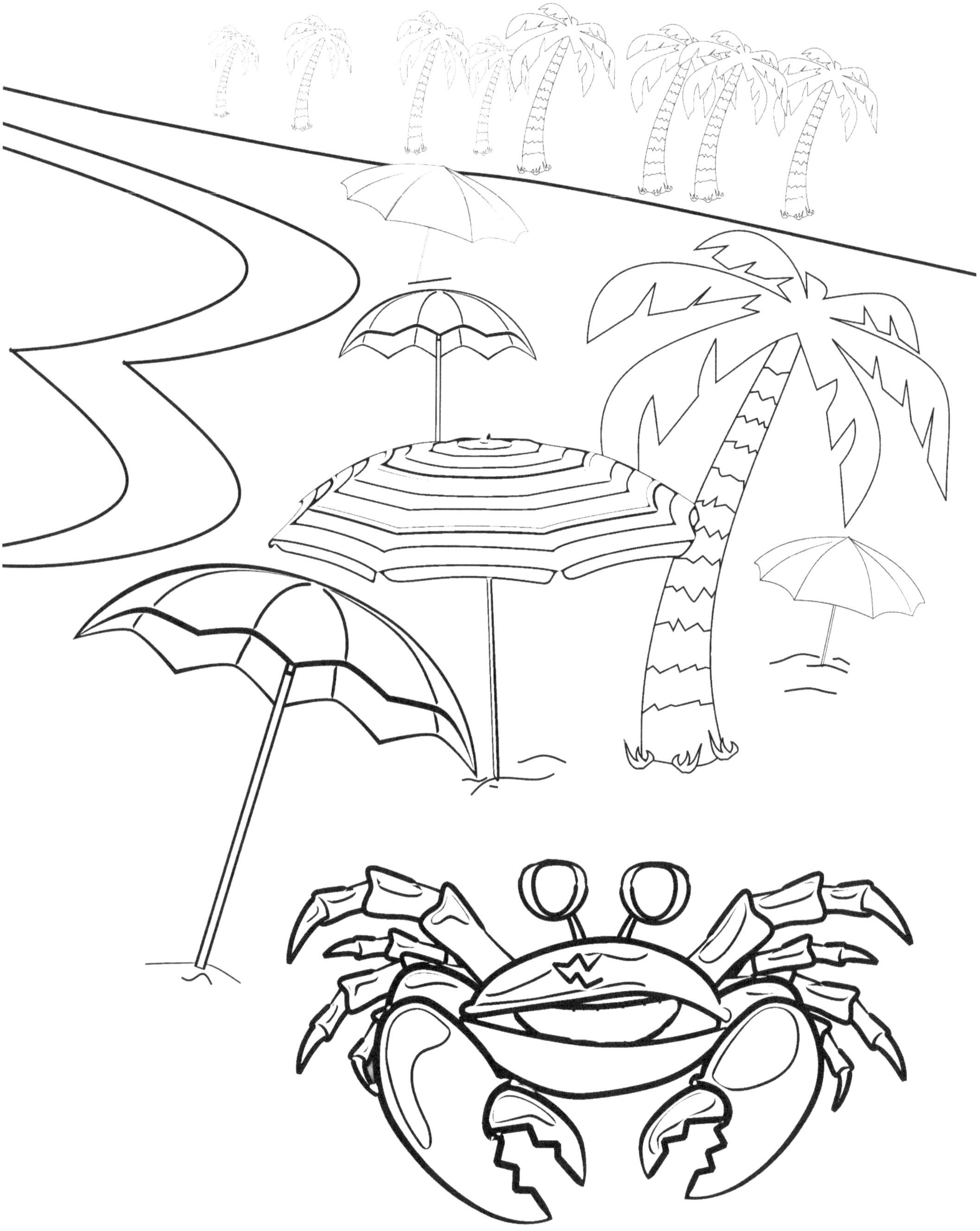

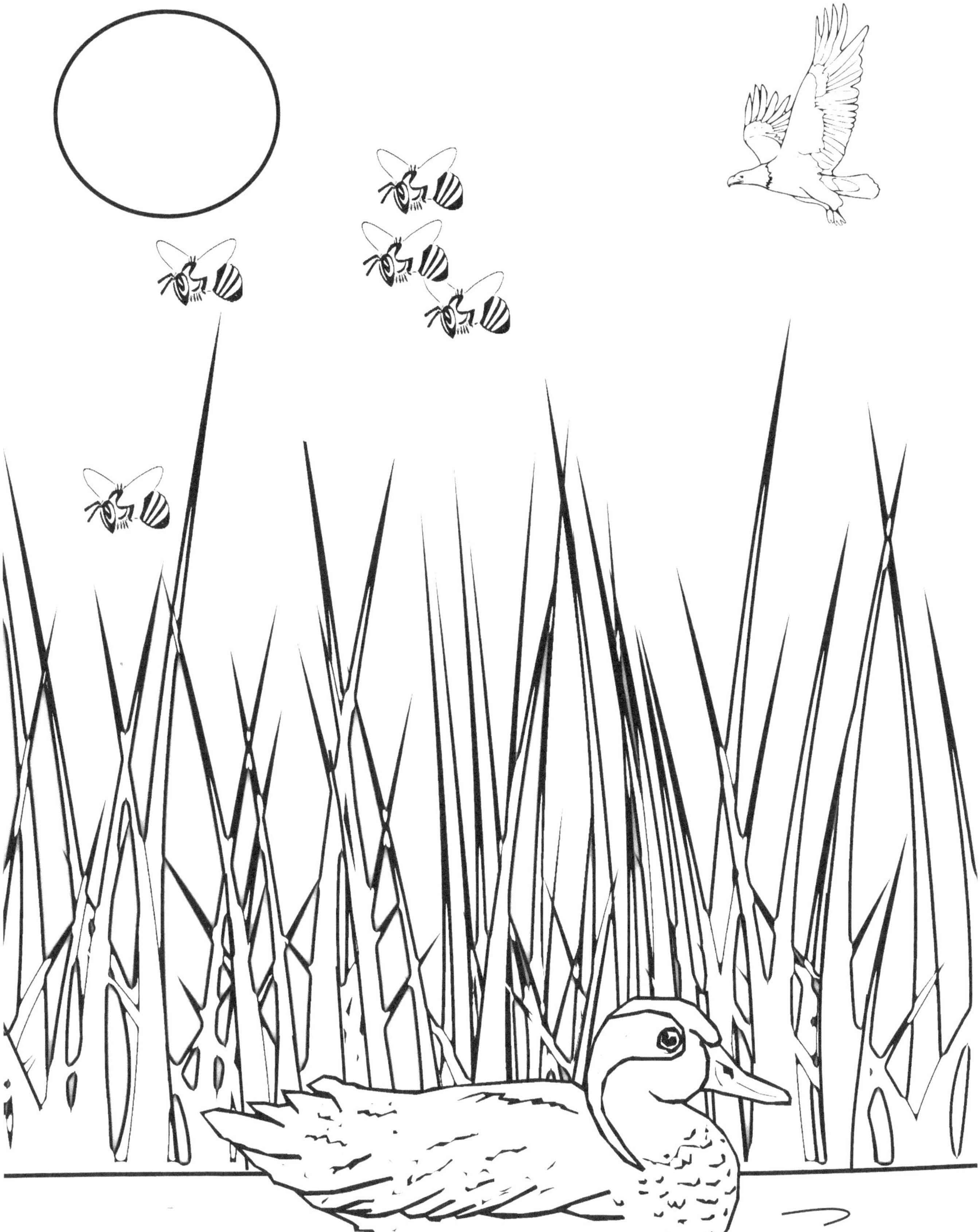

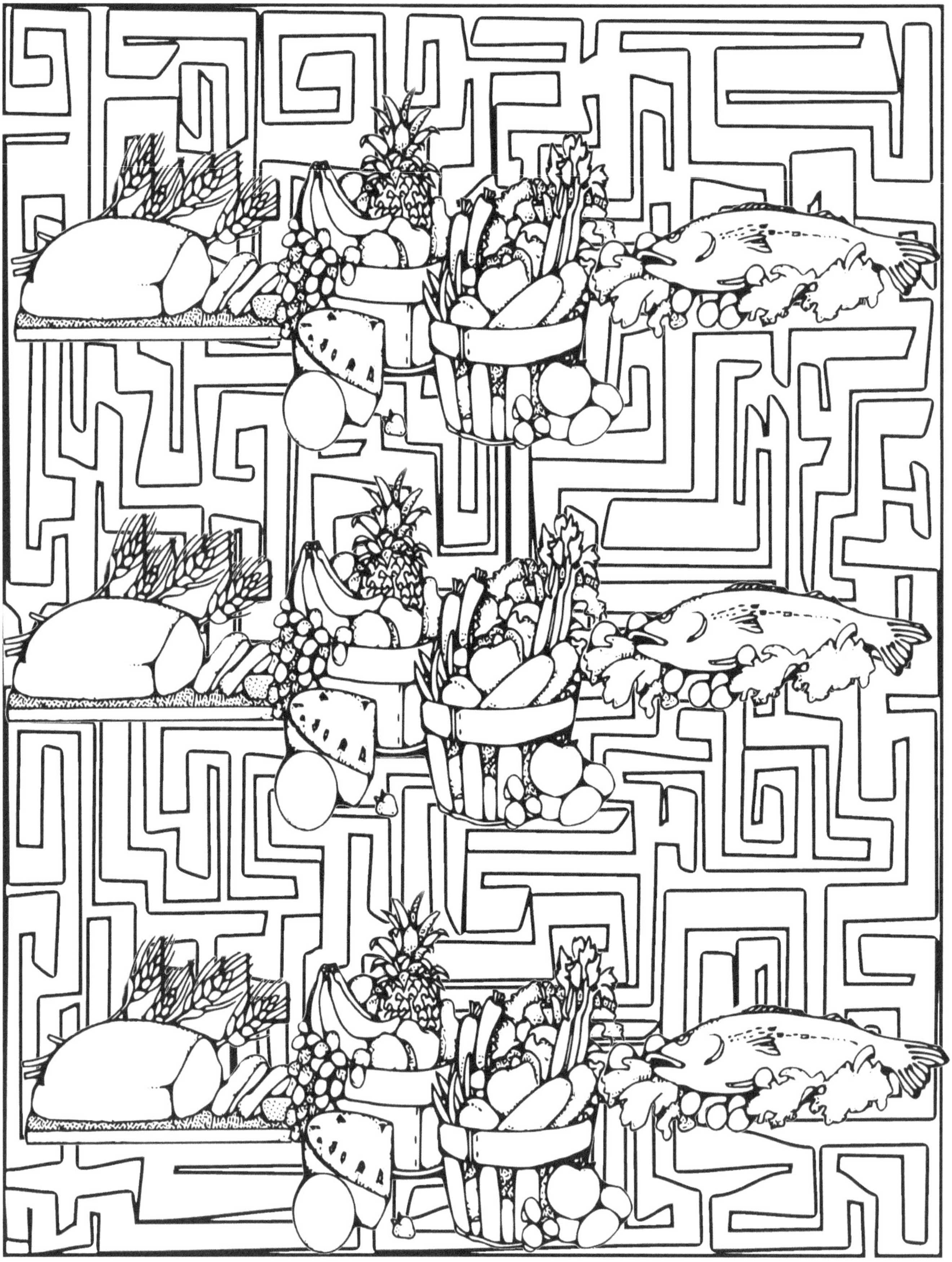

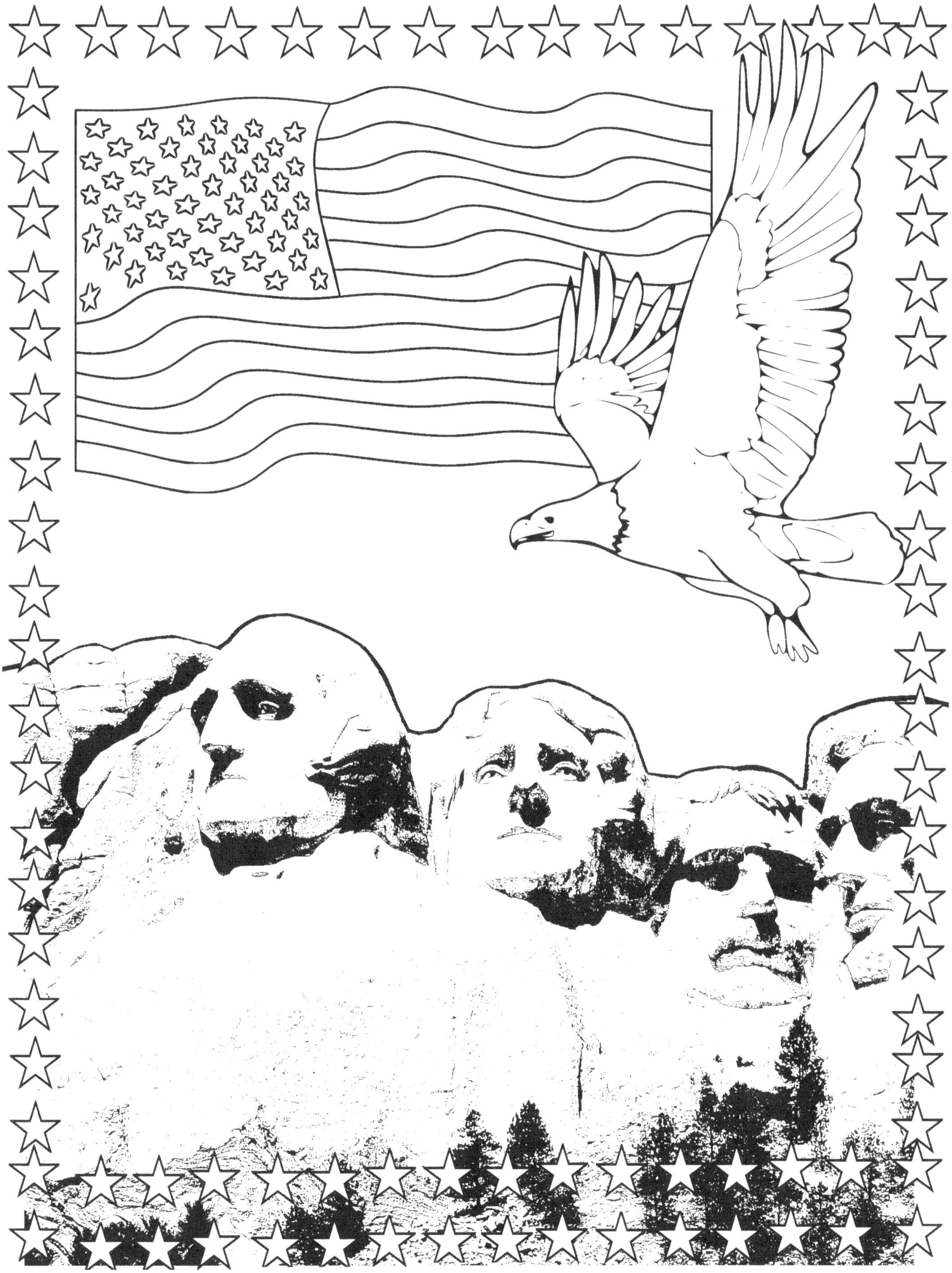

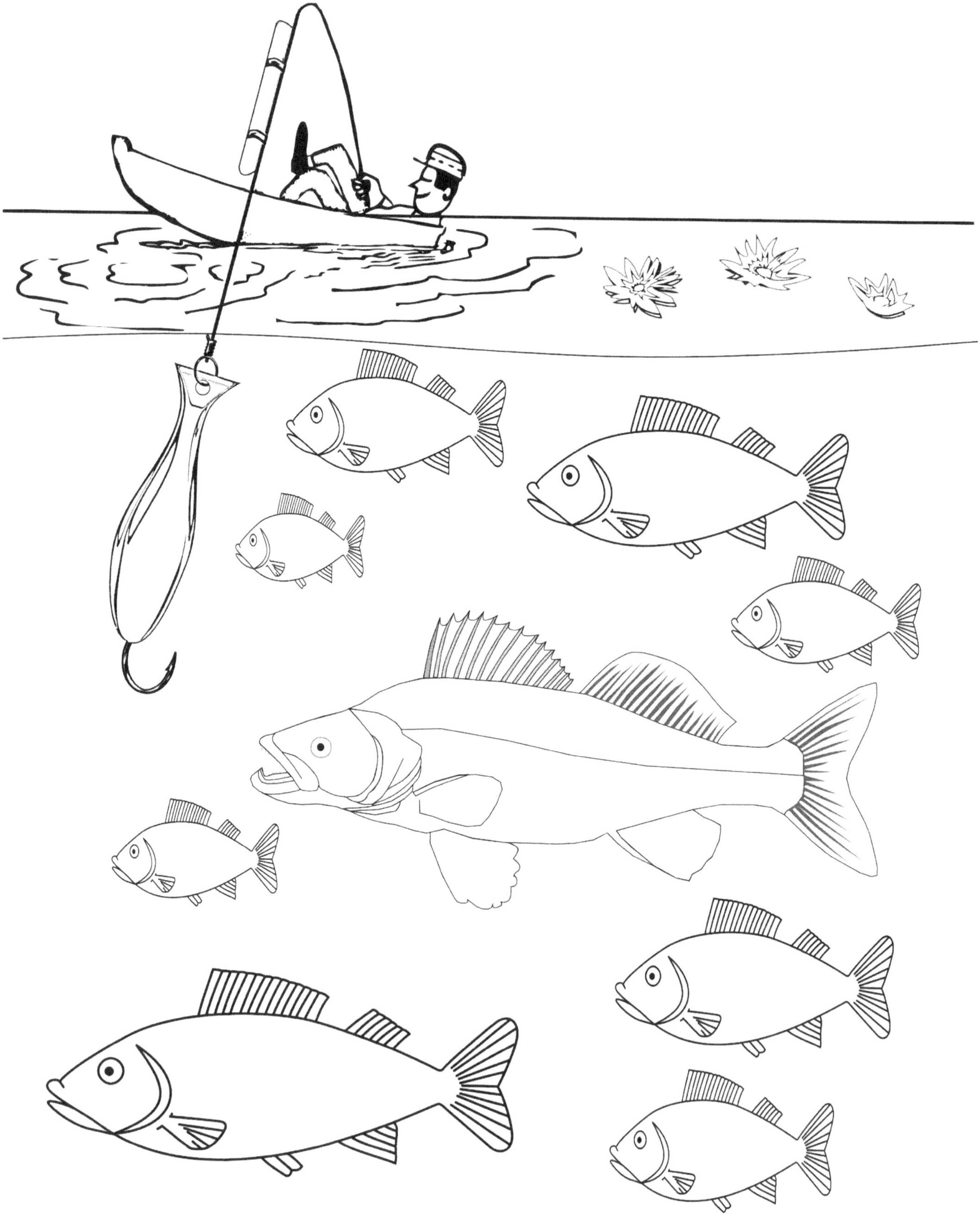

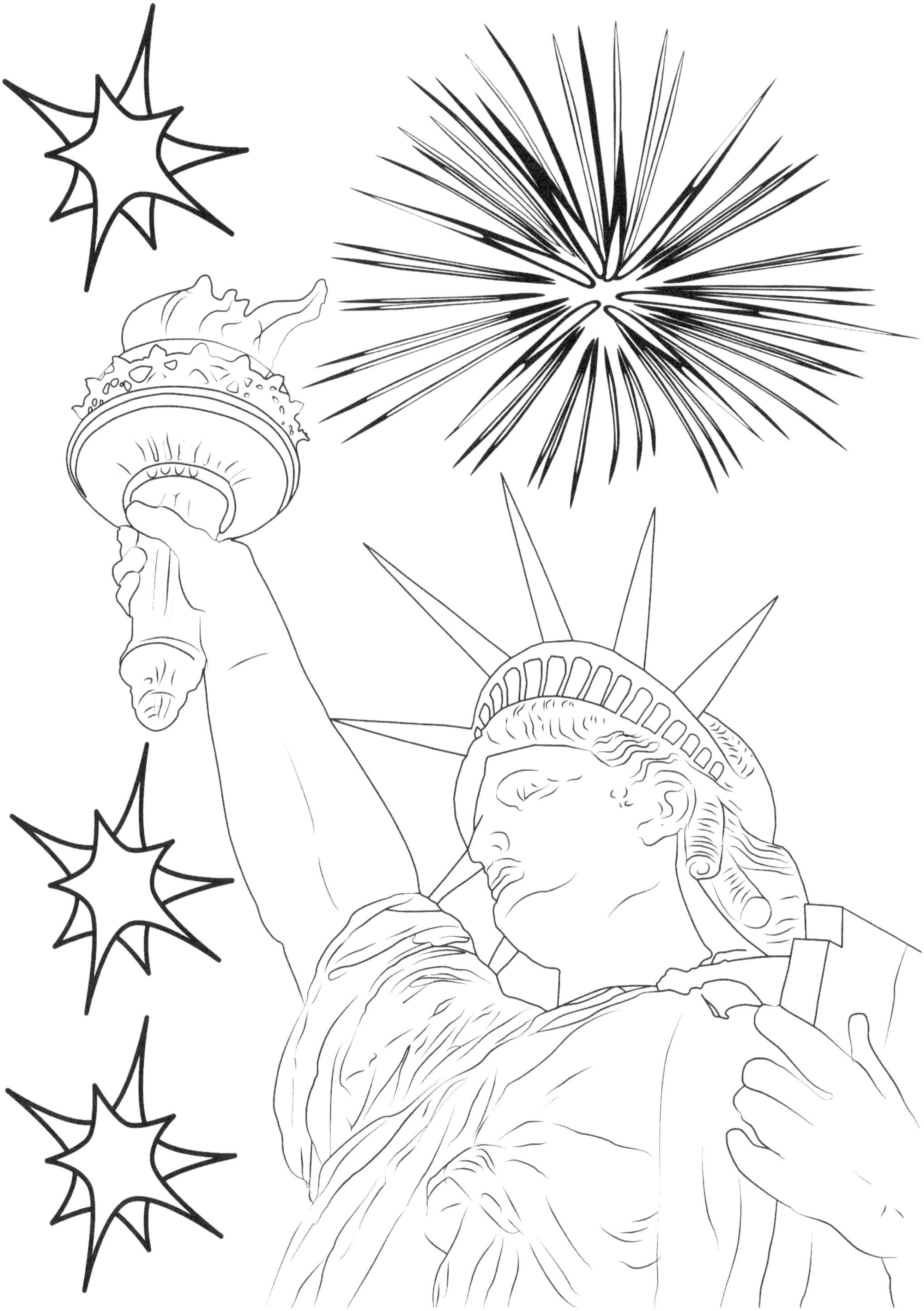

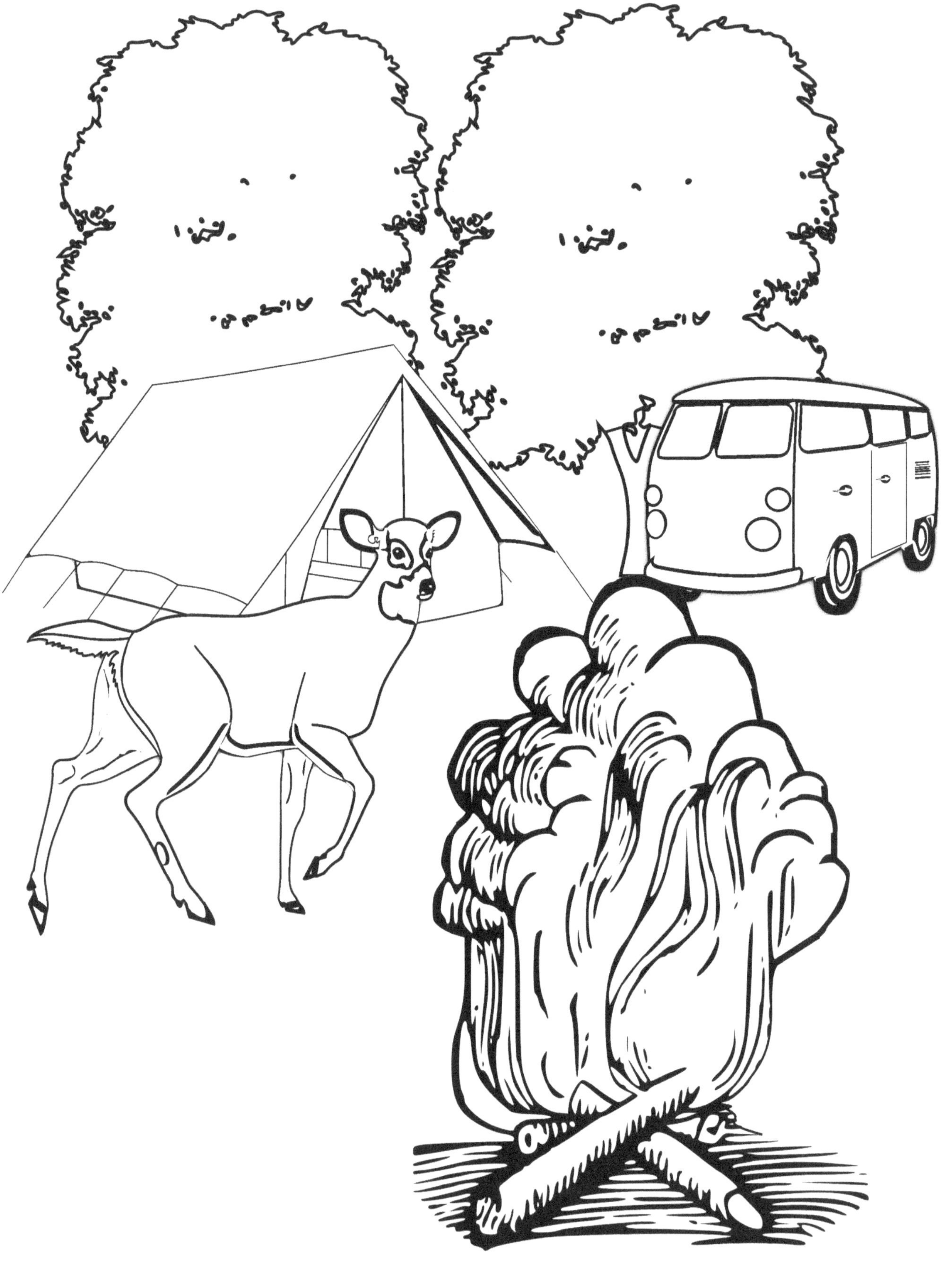

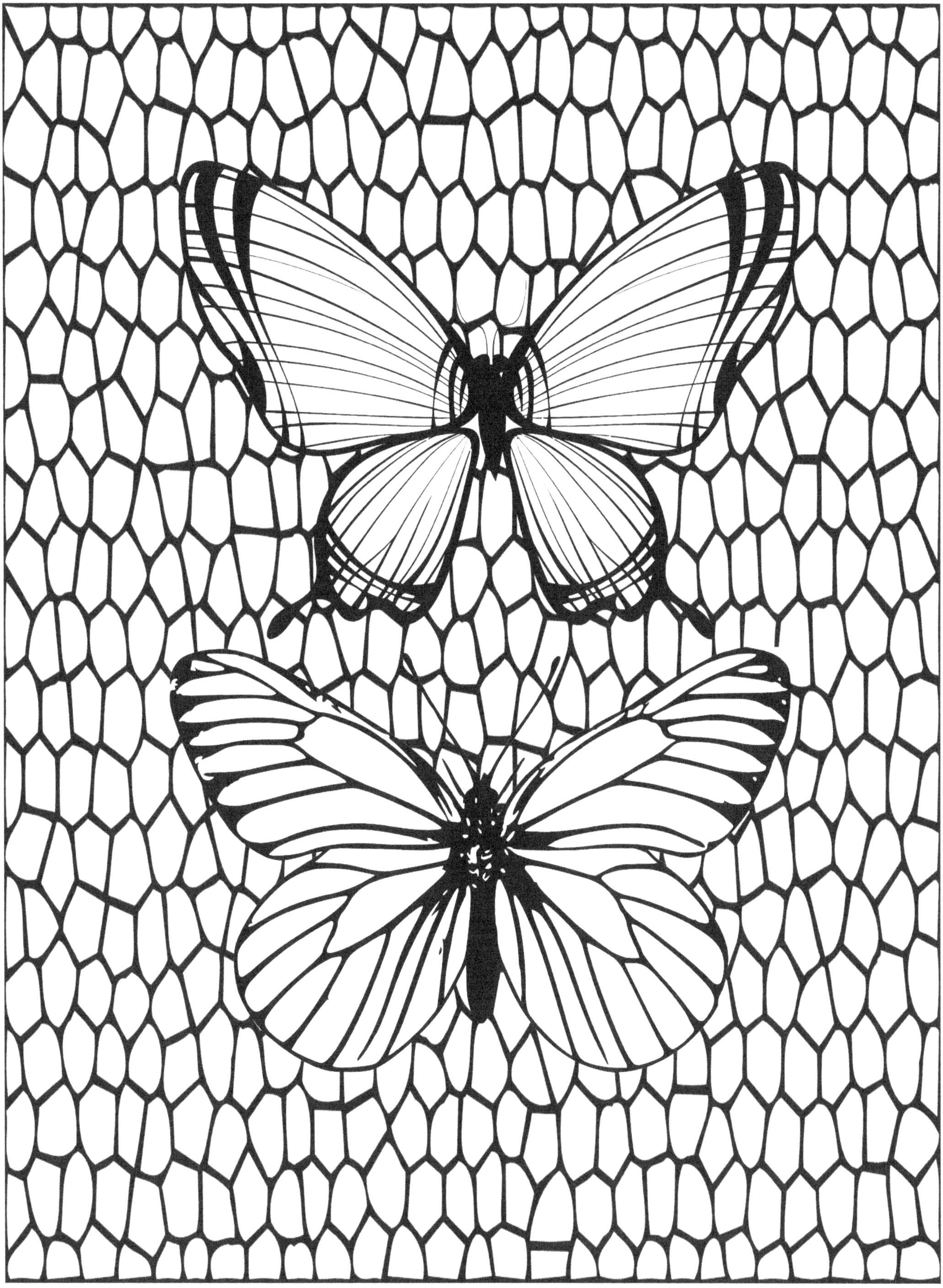

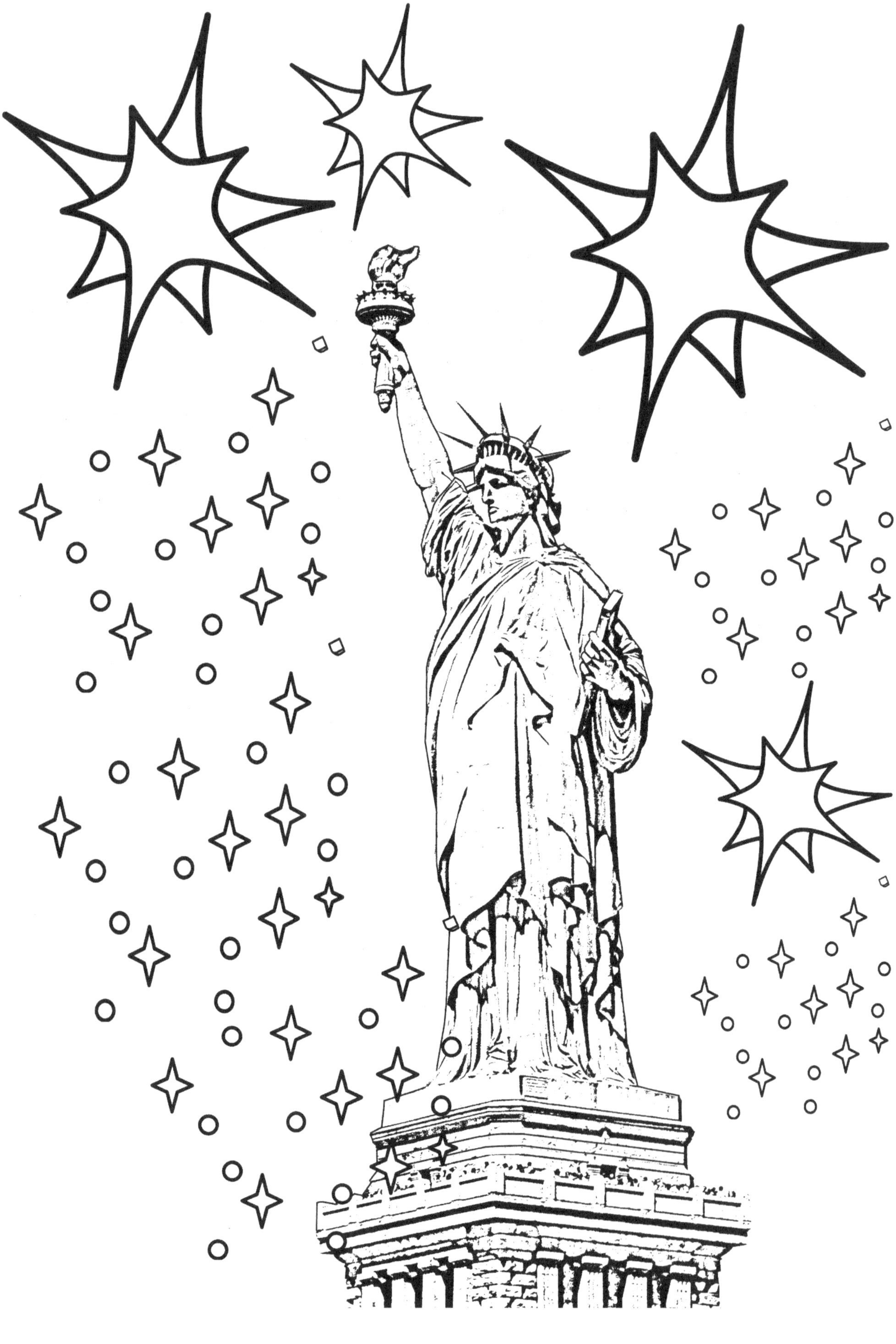

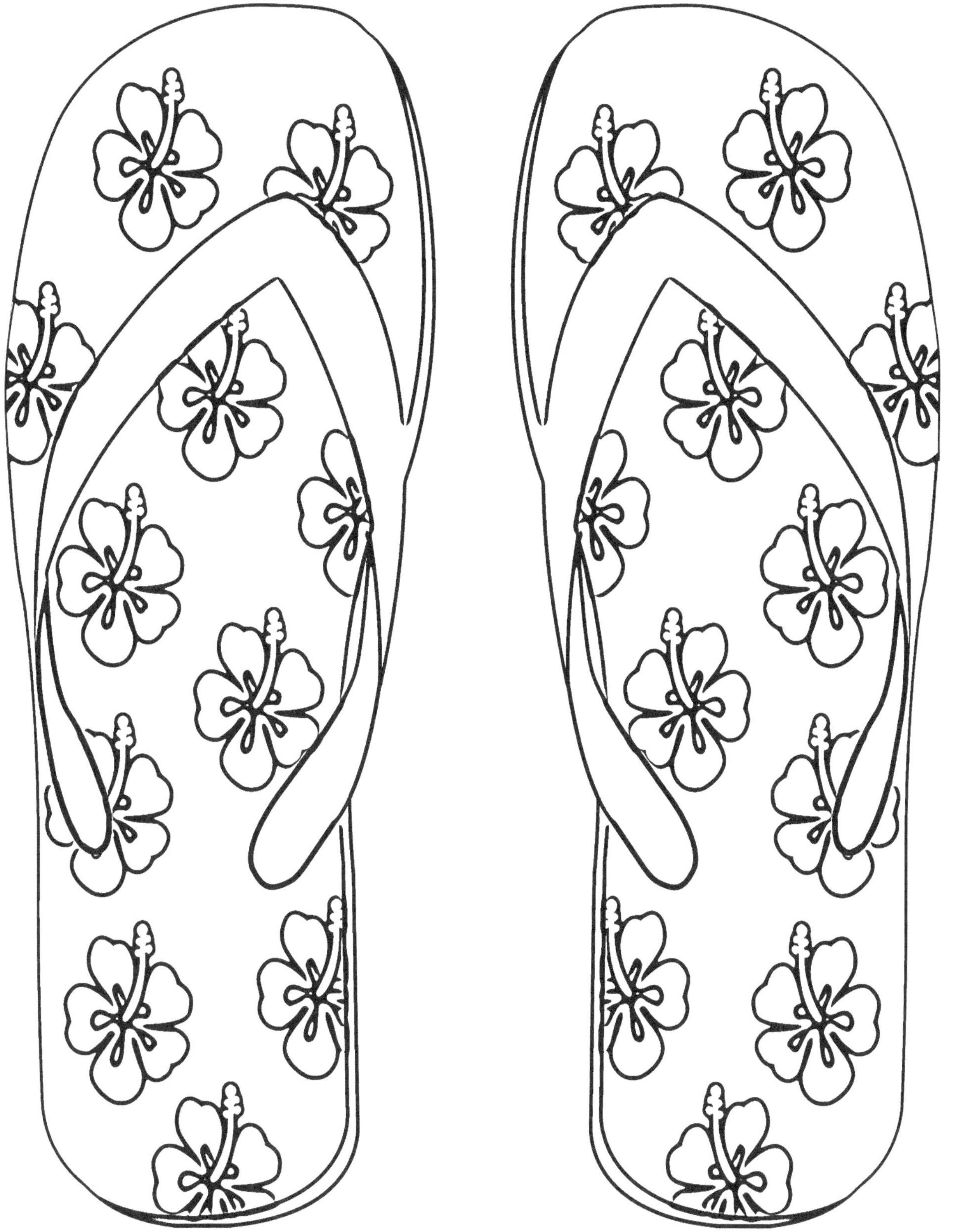

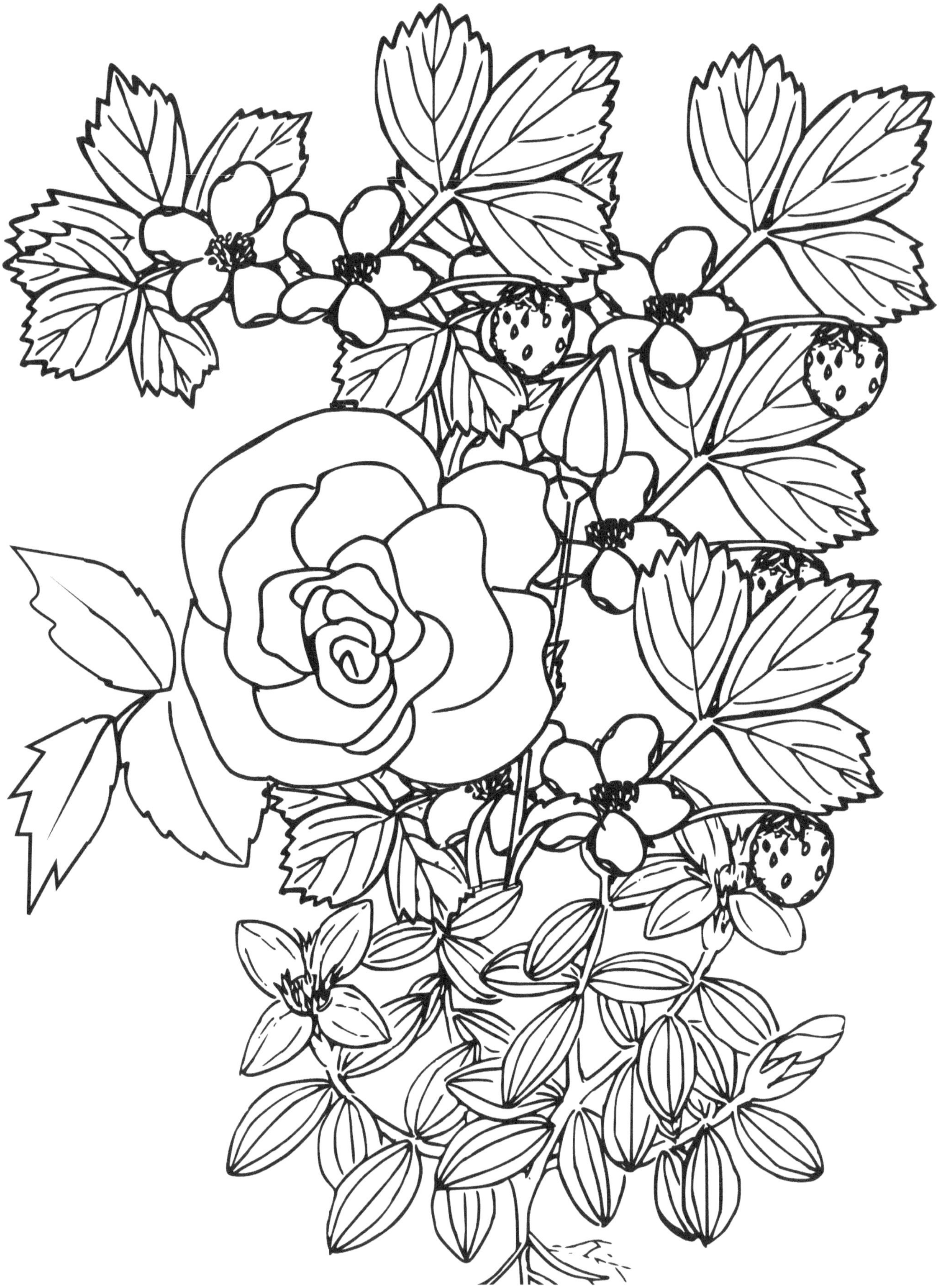

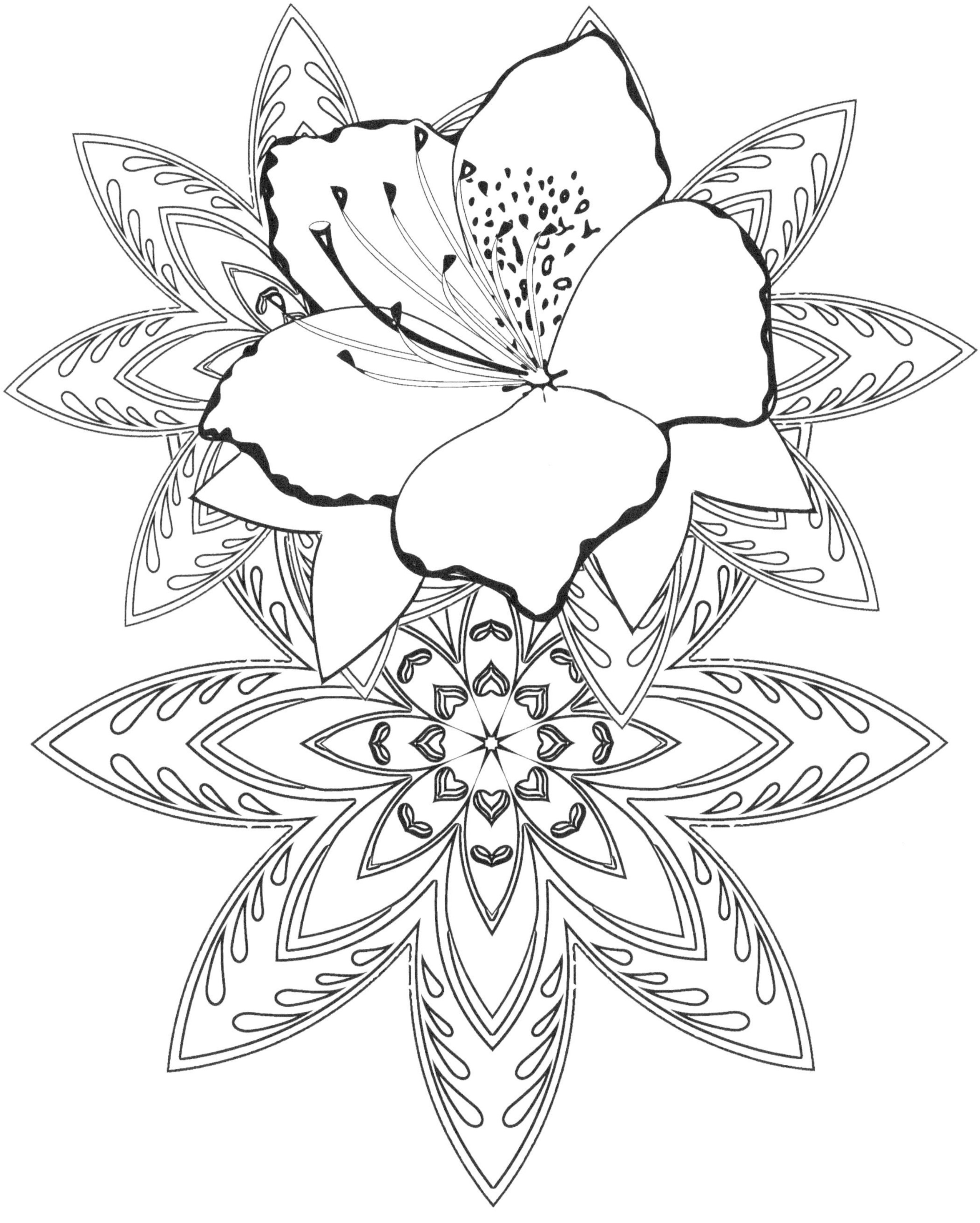

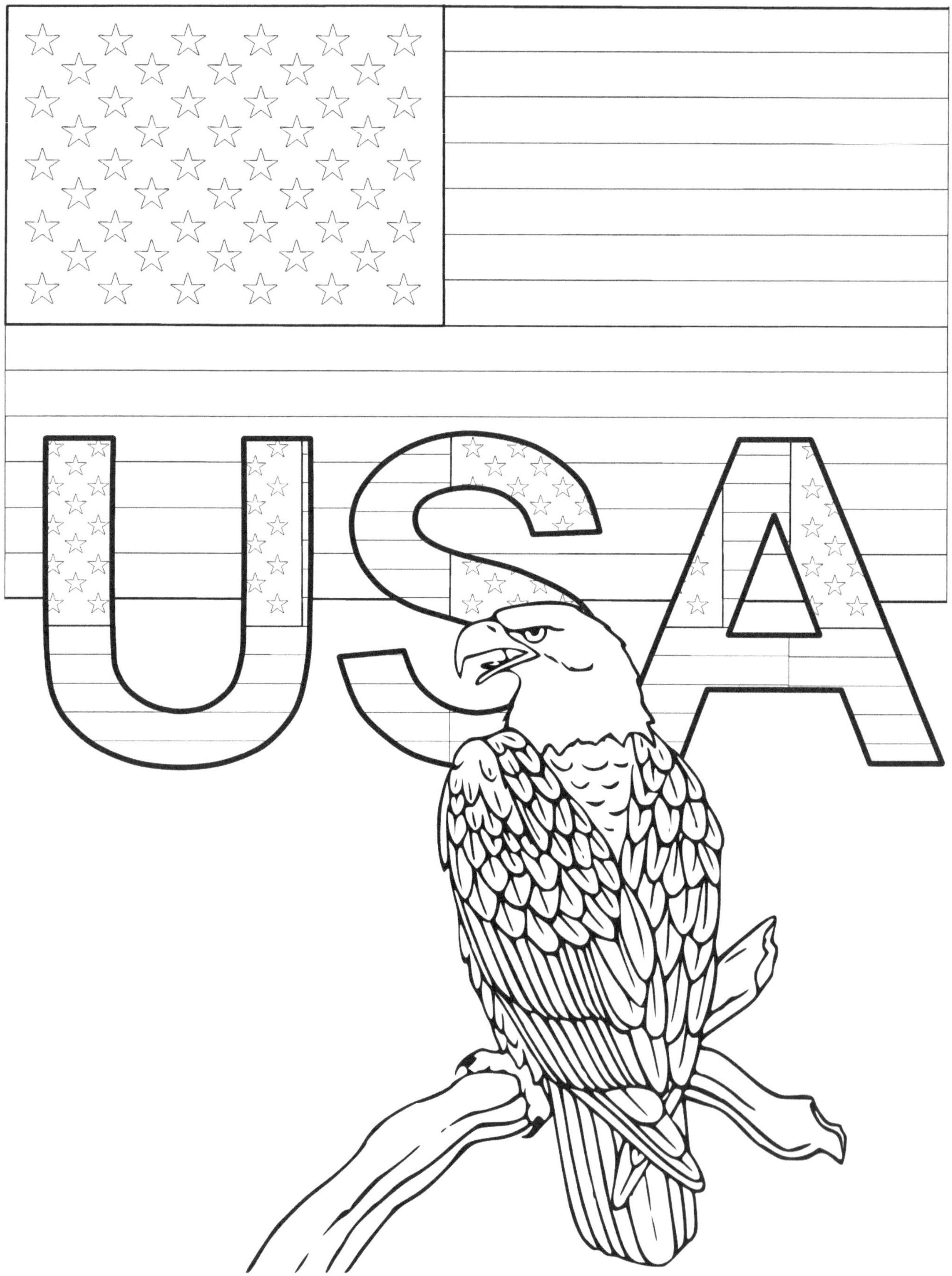
USA

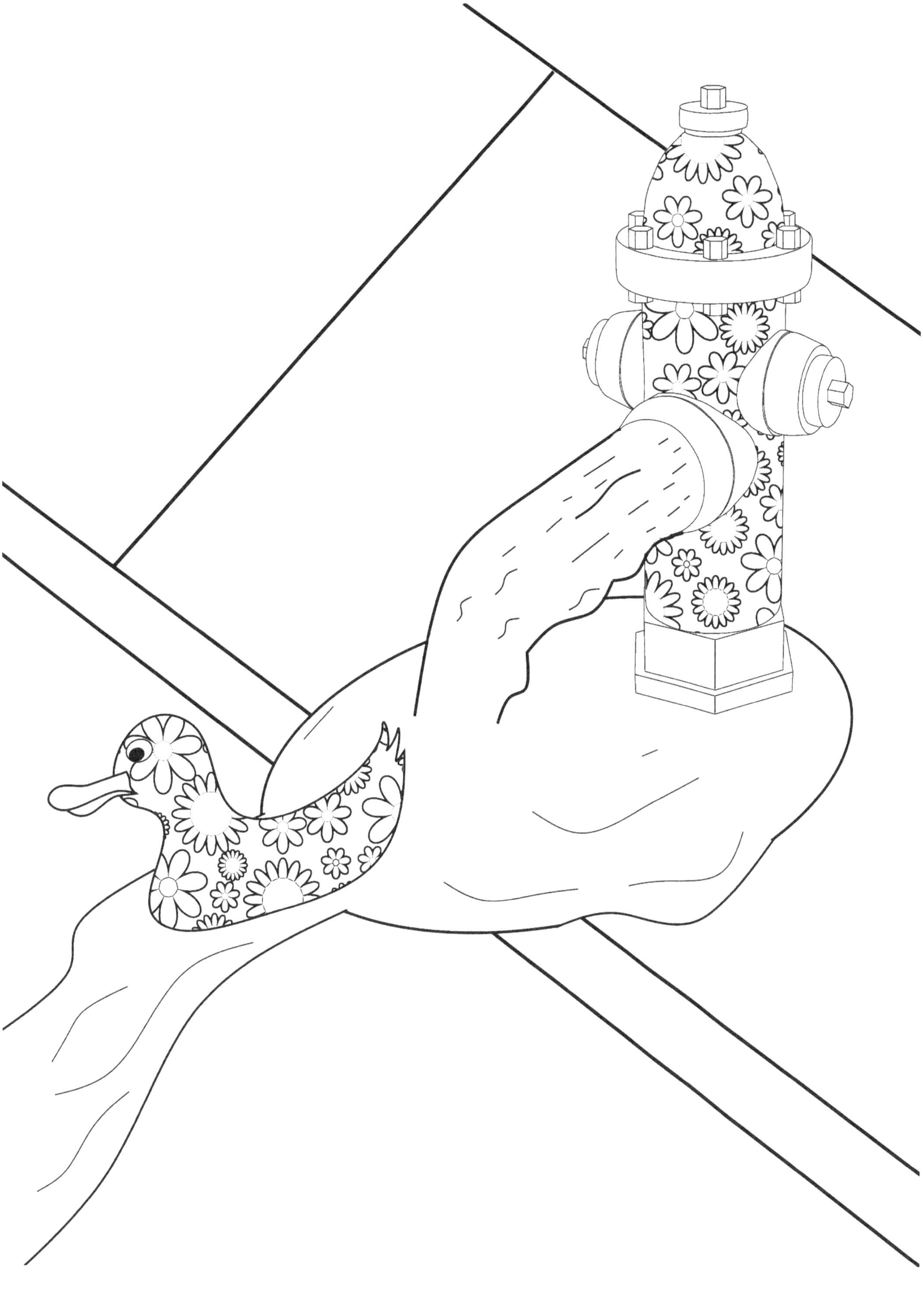

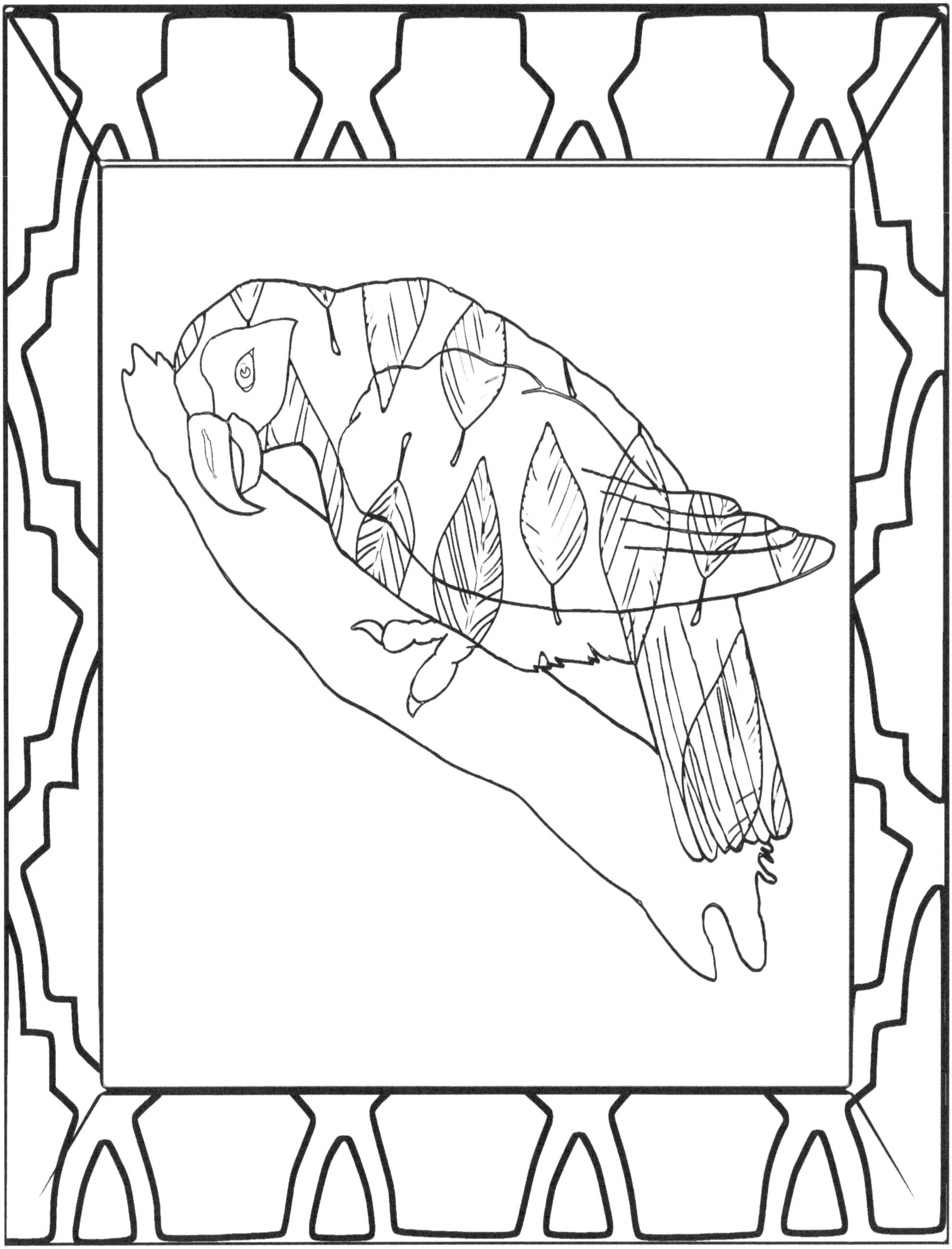

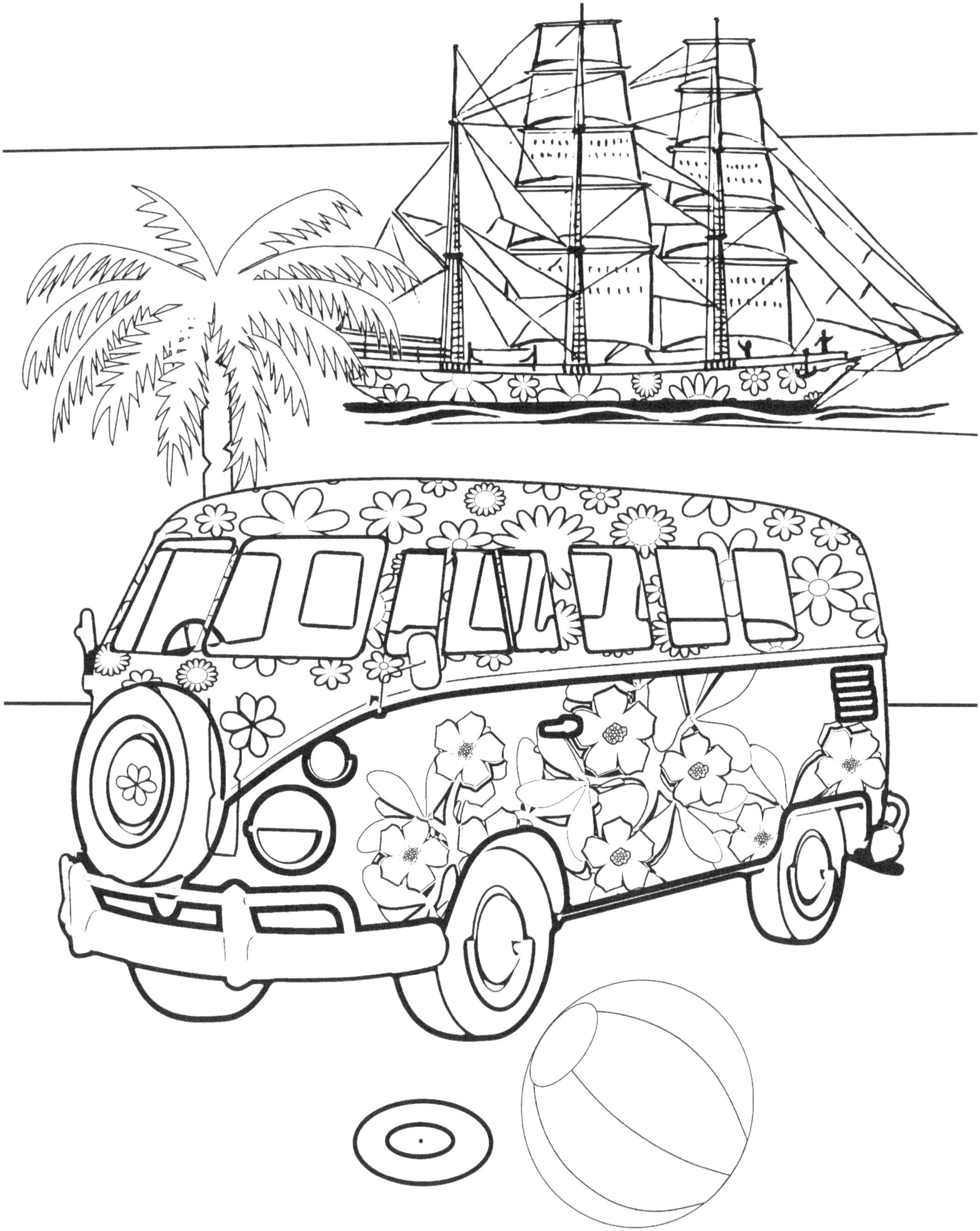

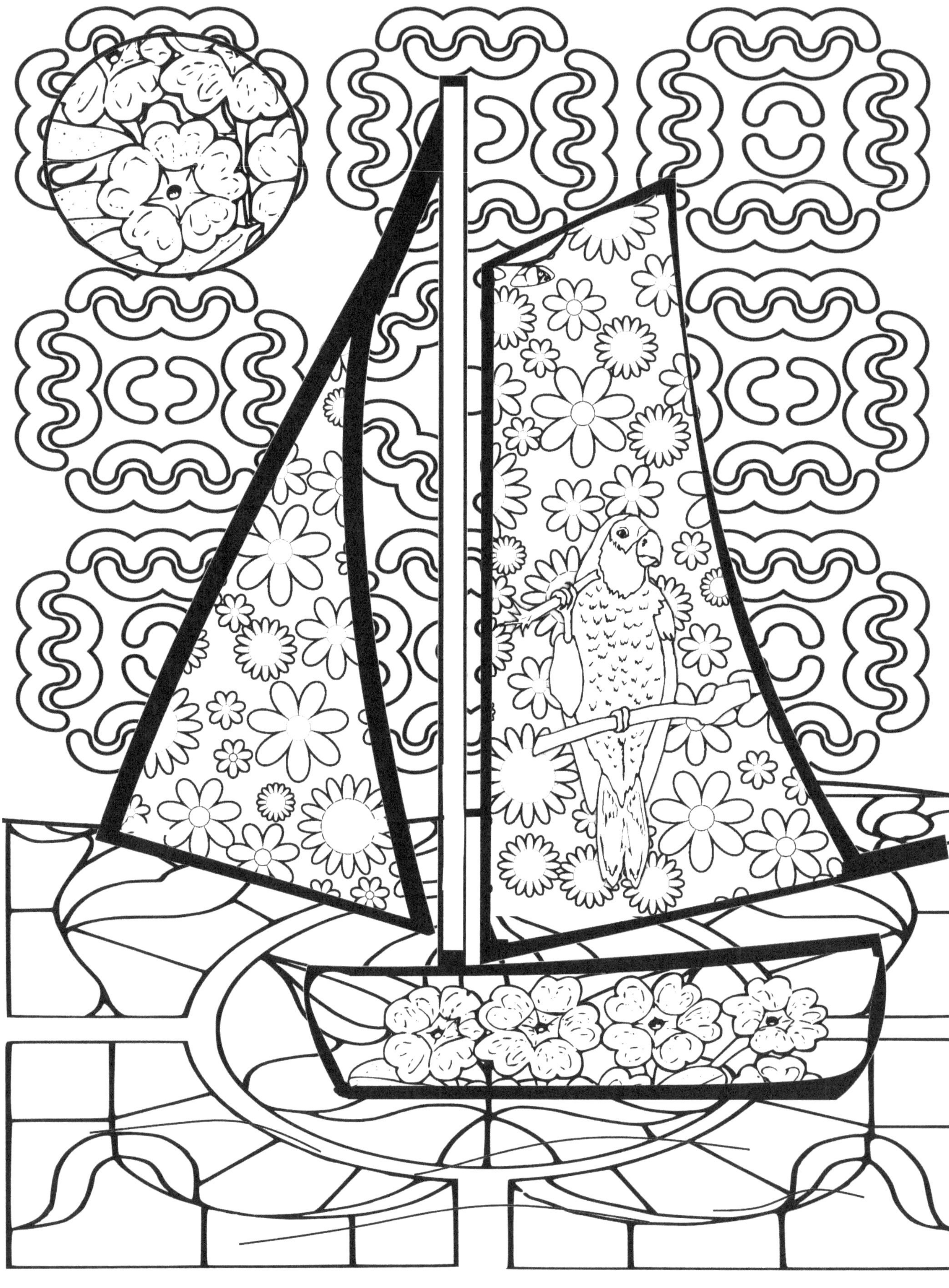

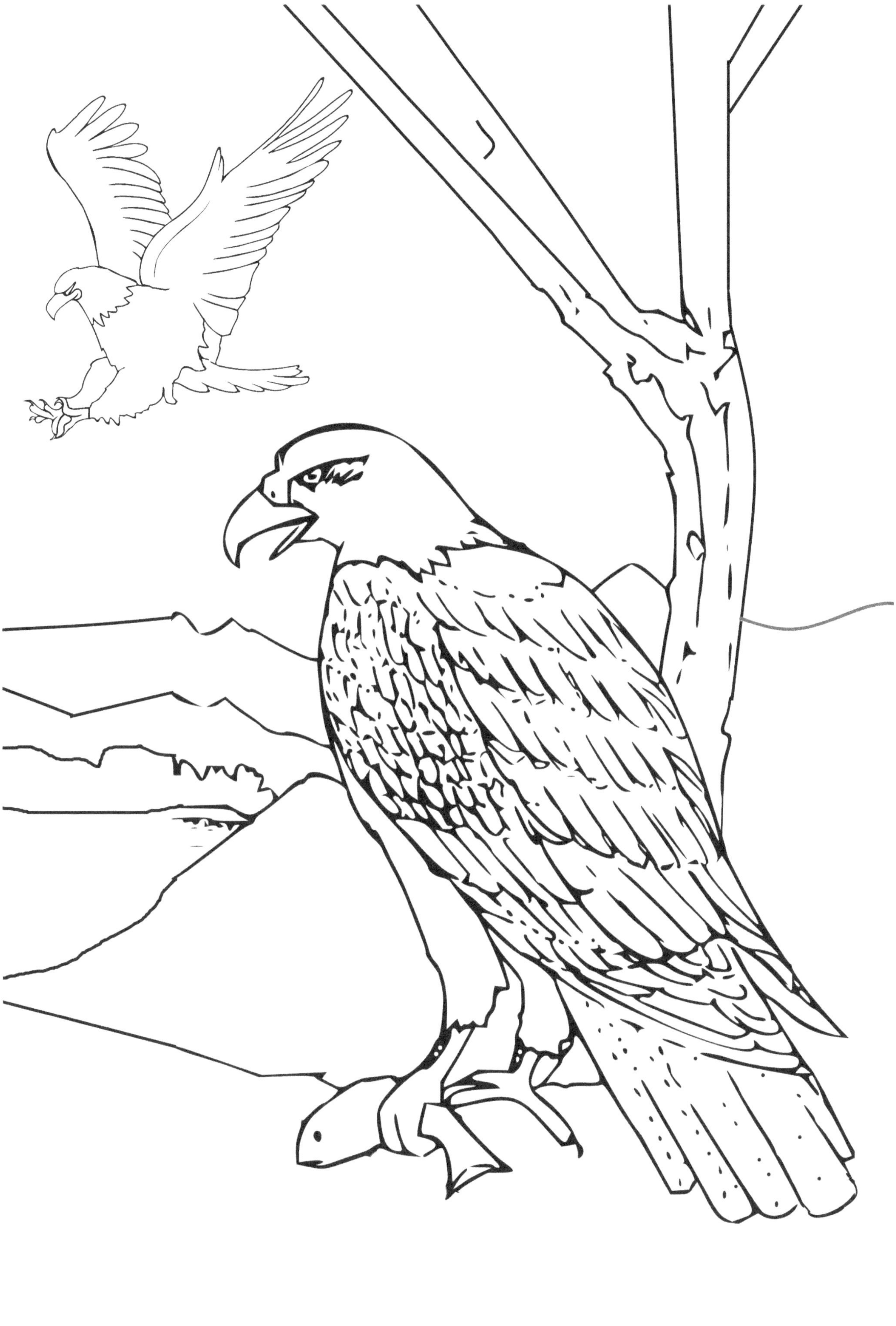

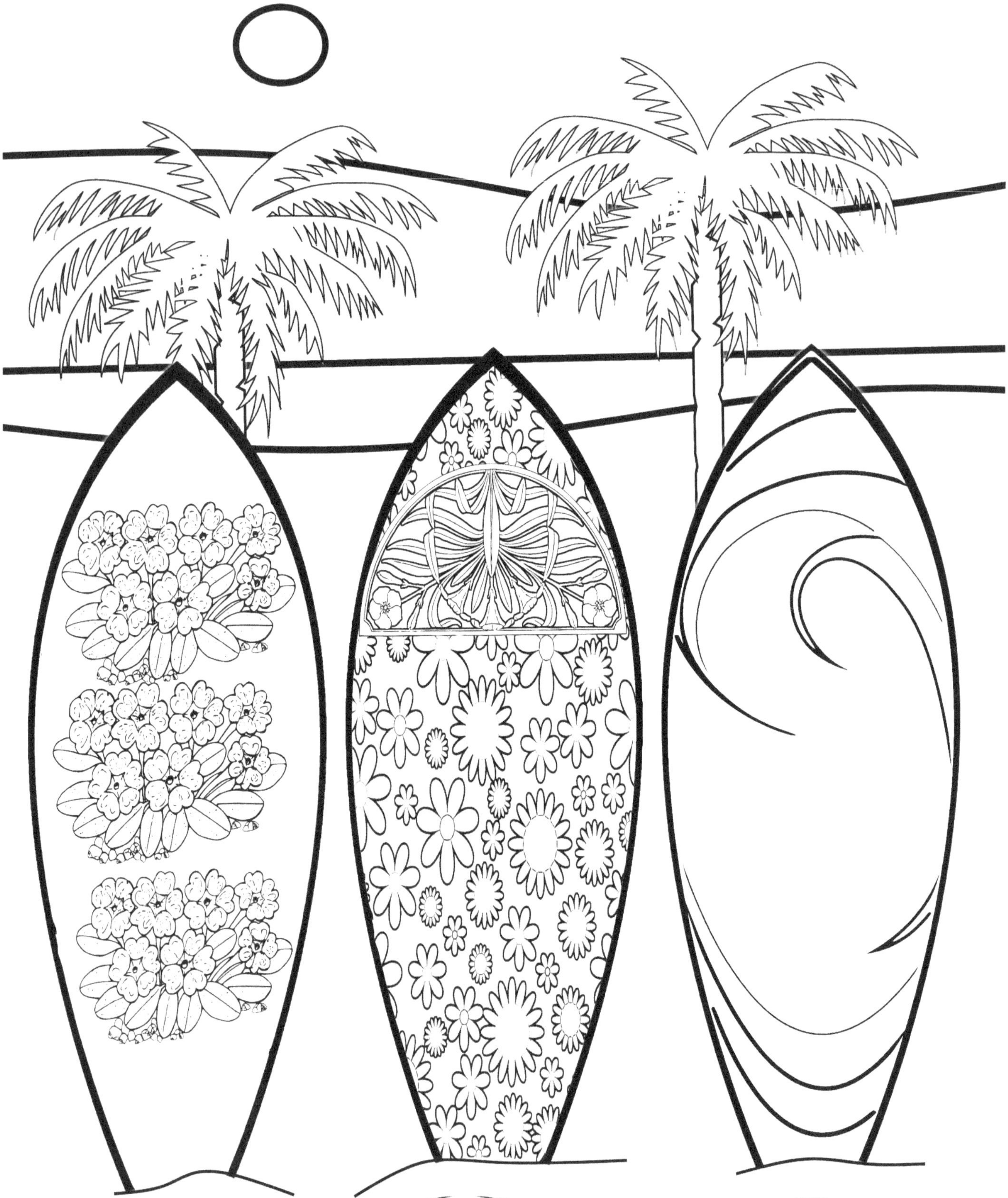

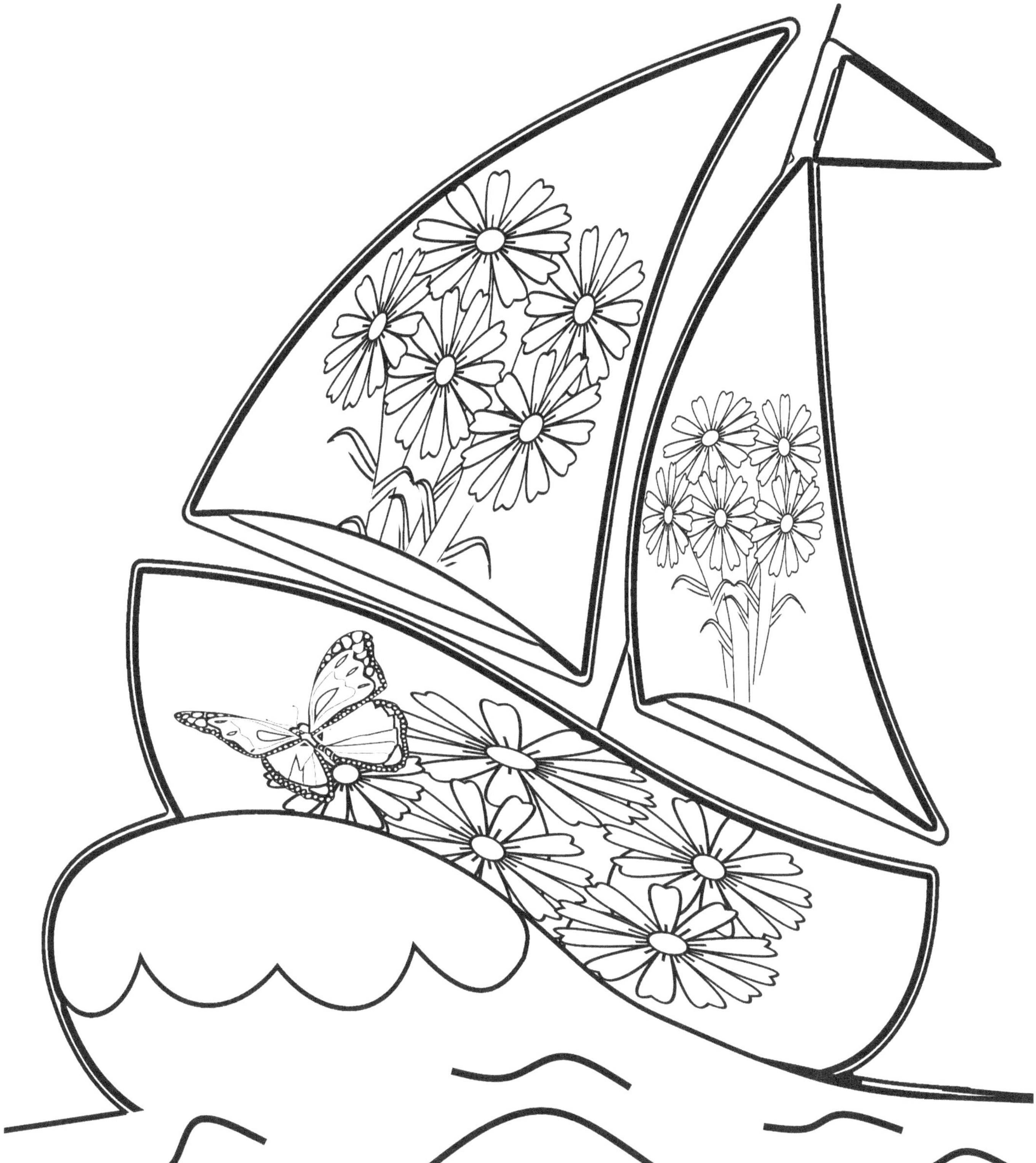

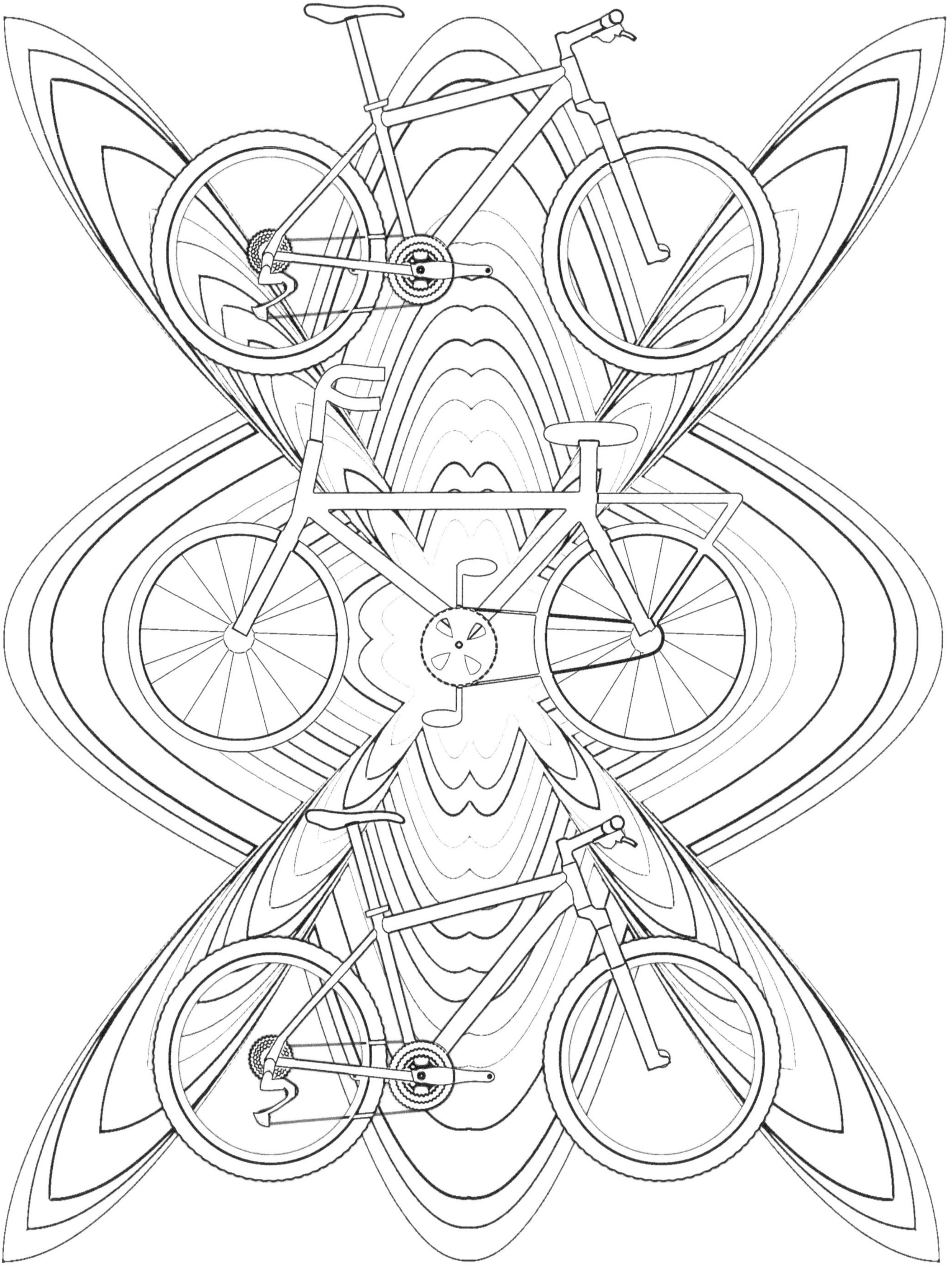

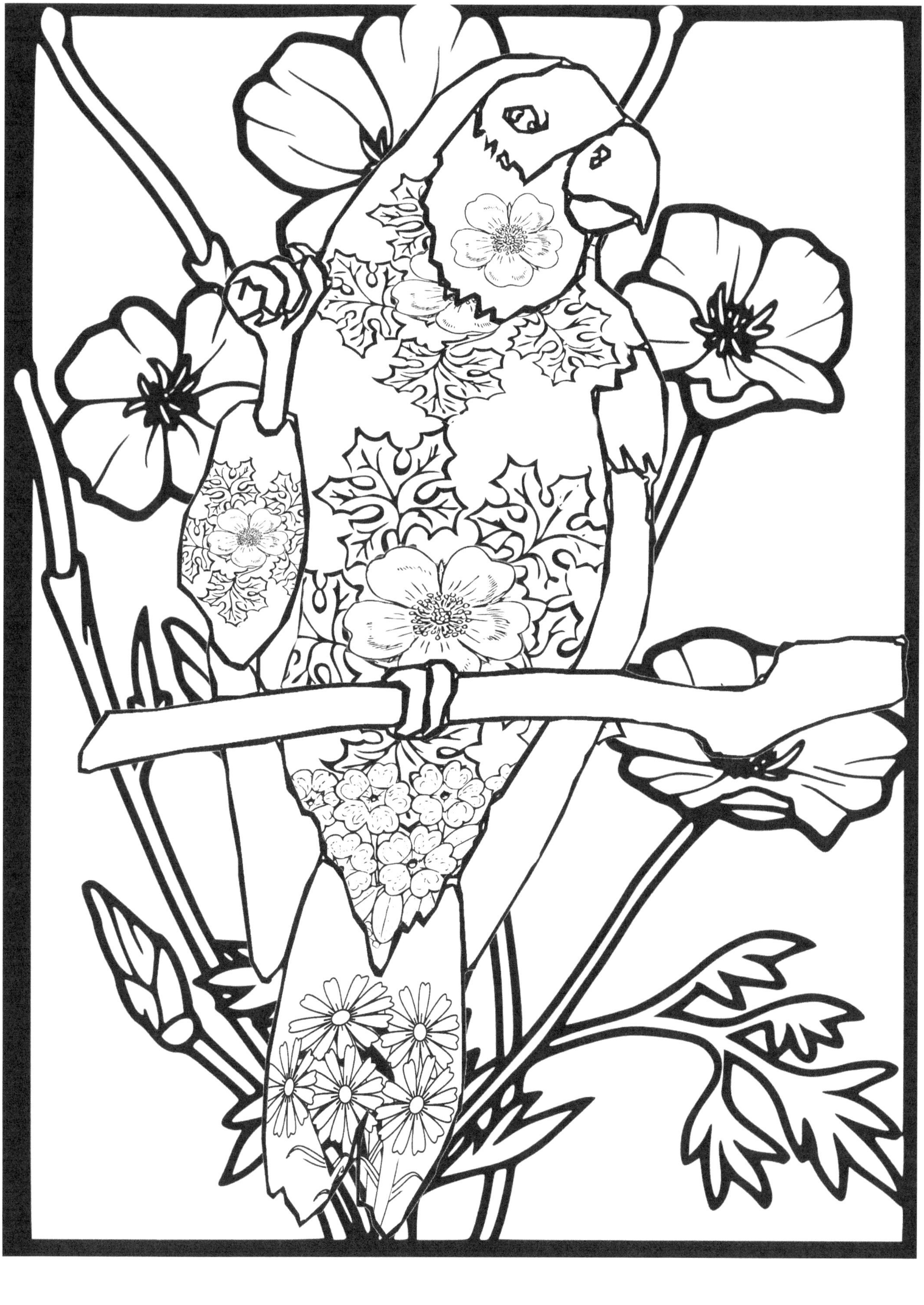

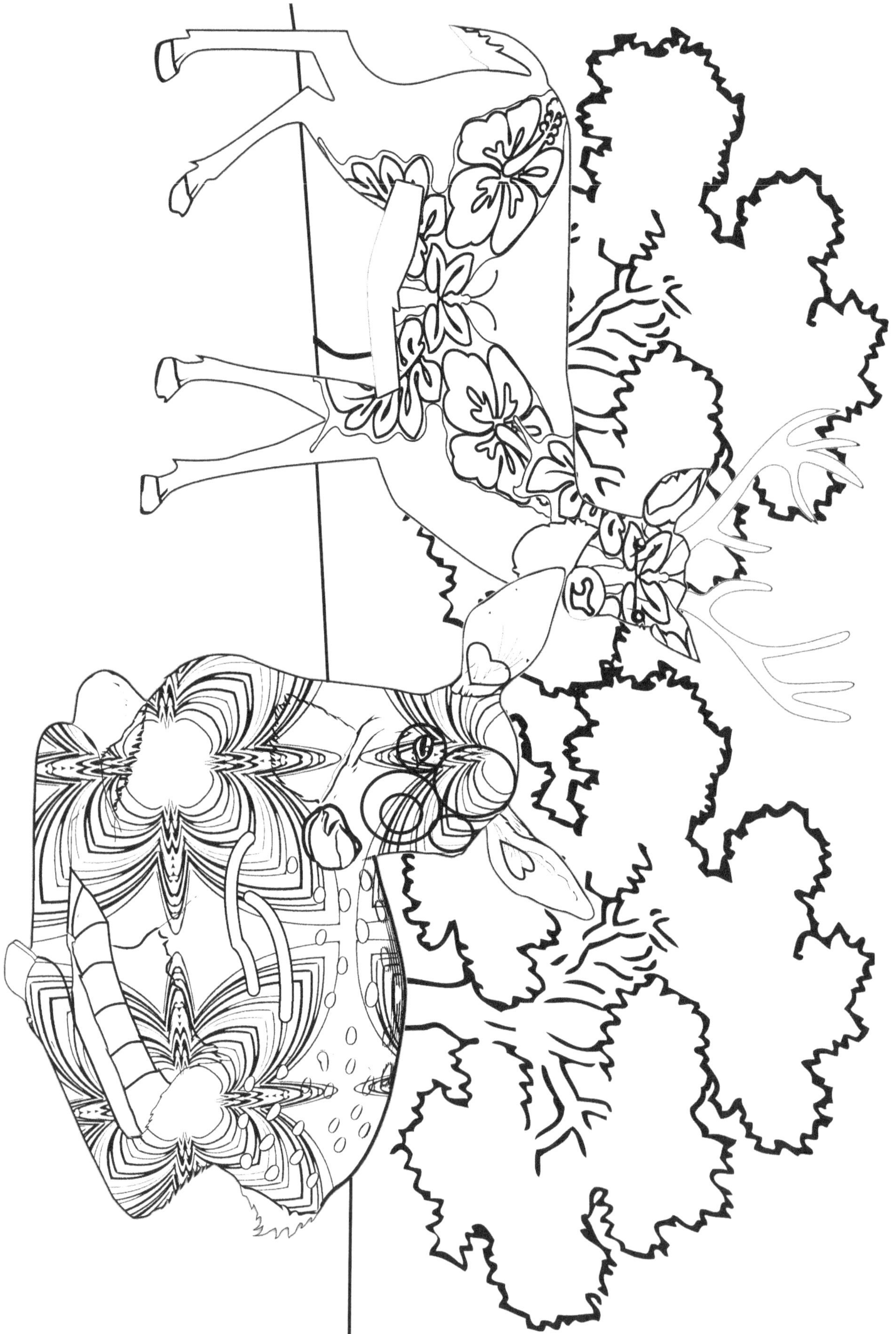

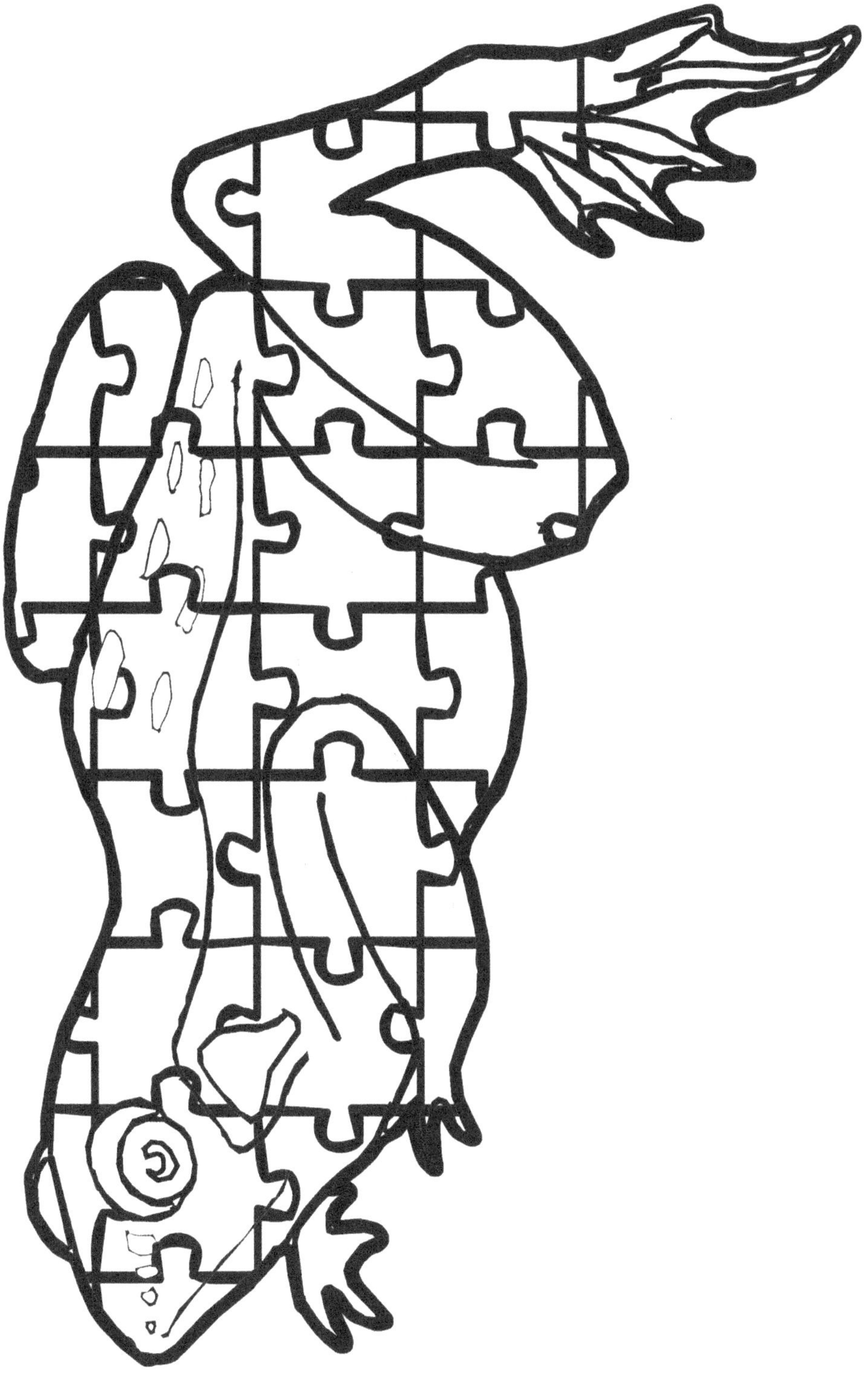

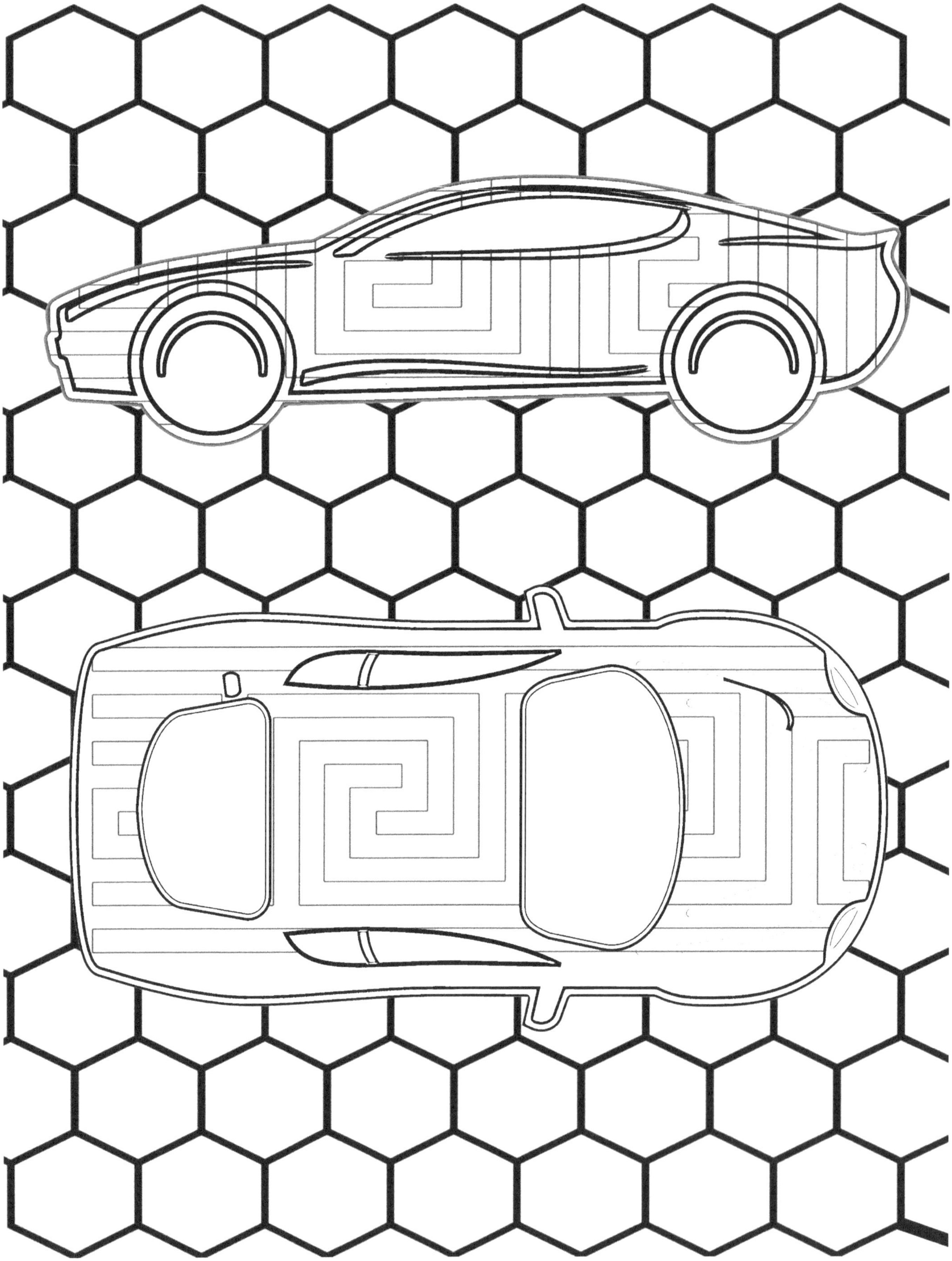

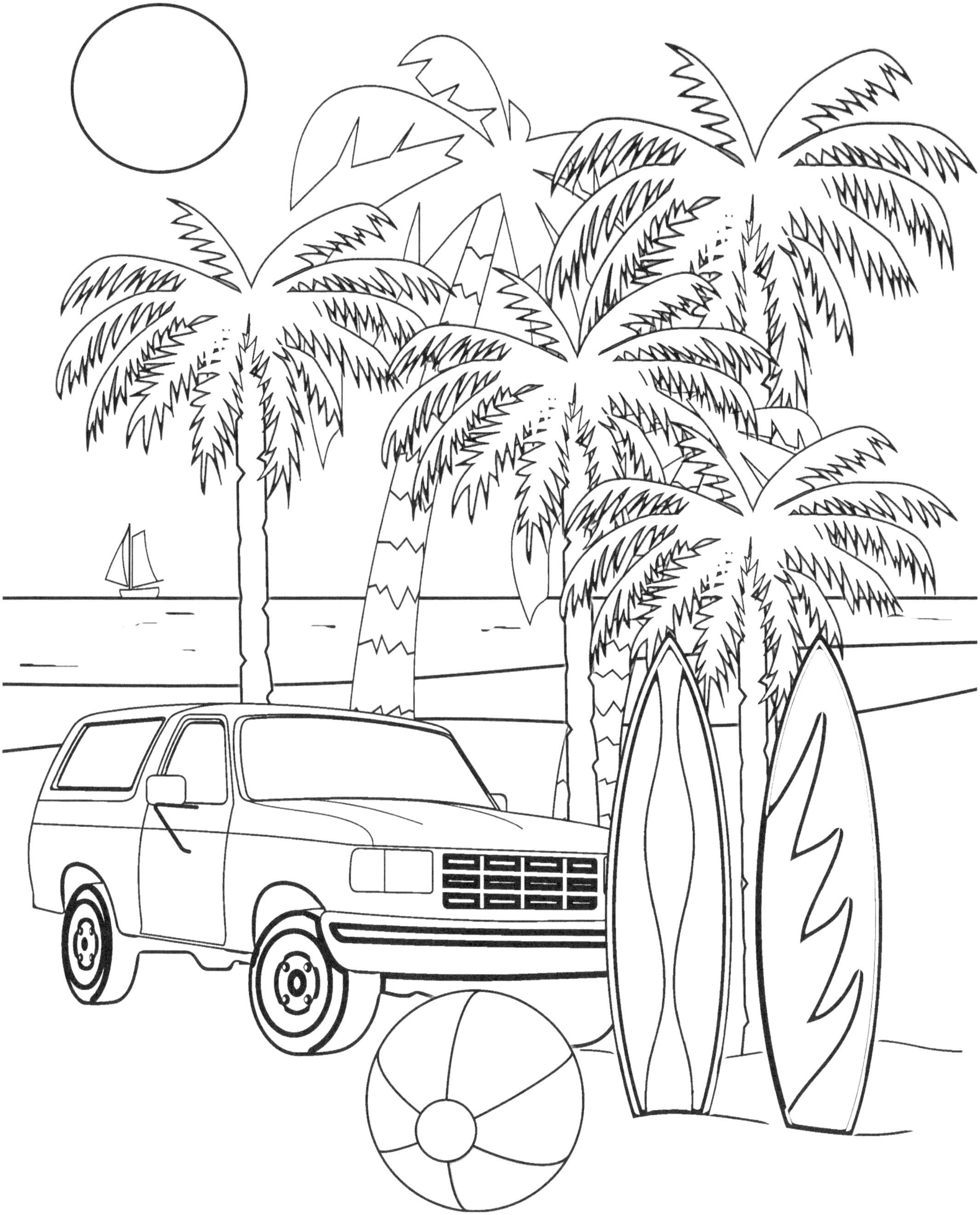

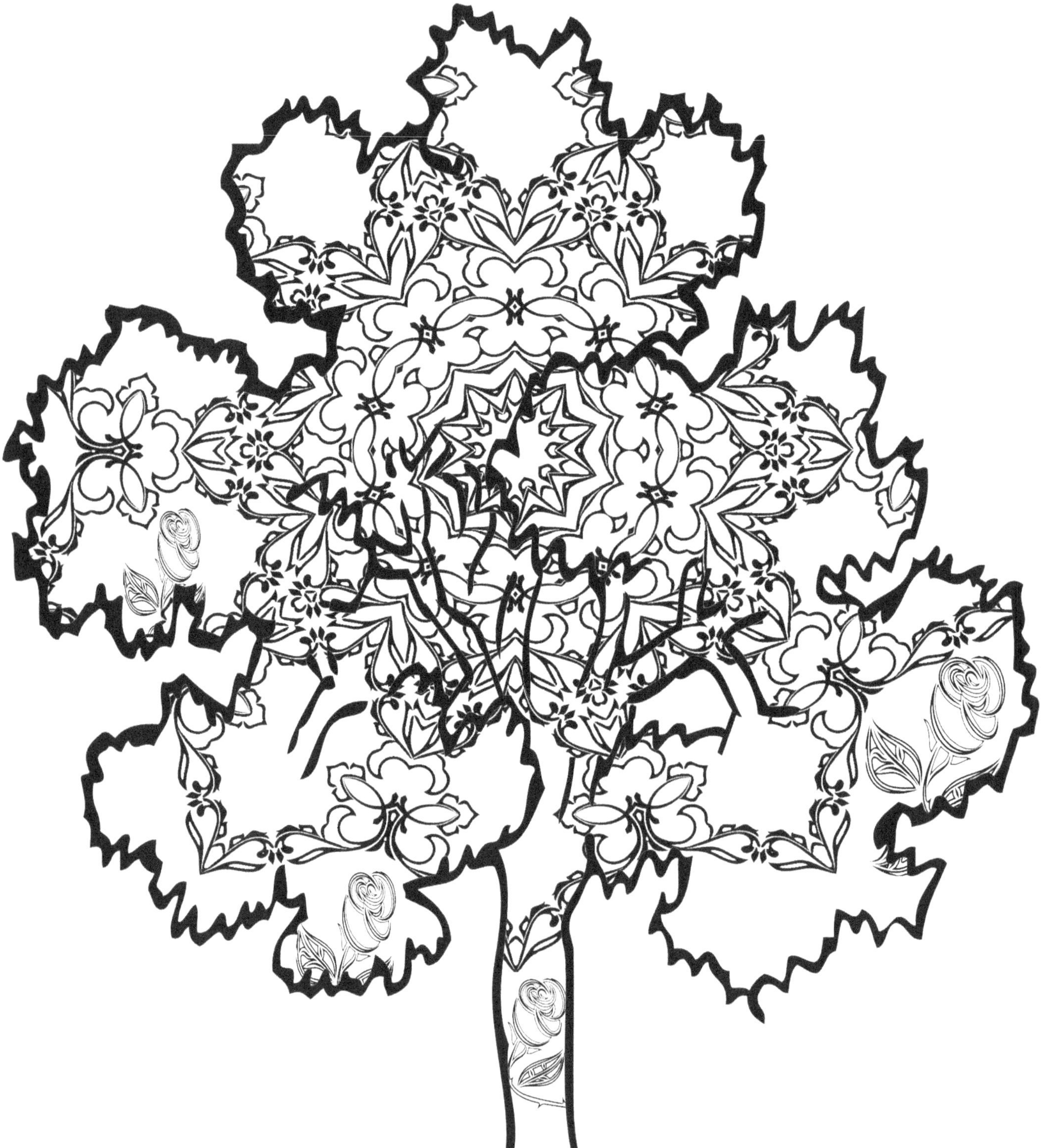

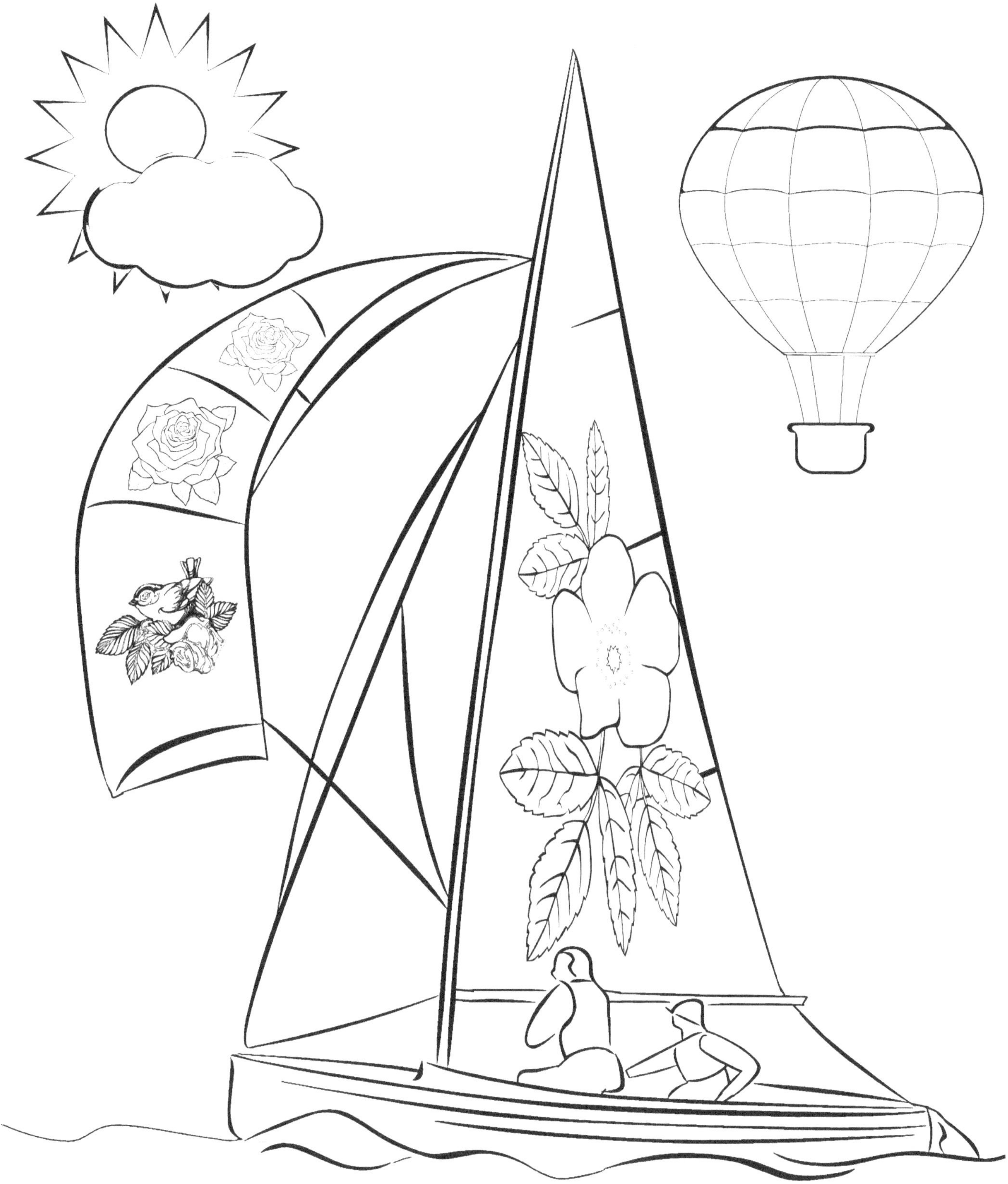

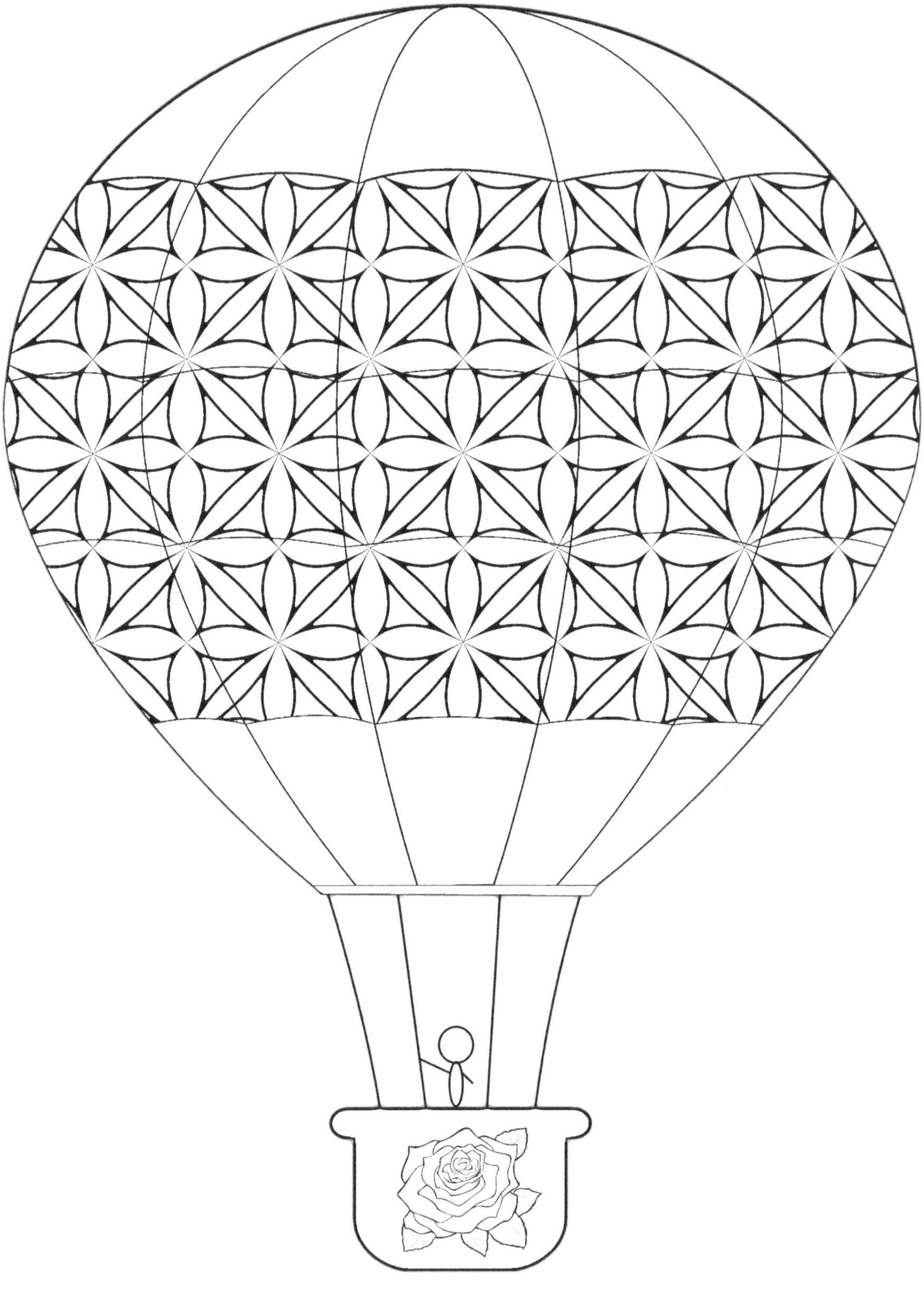

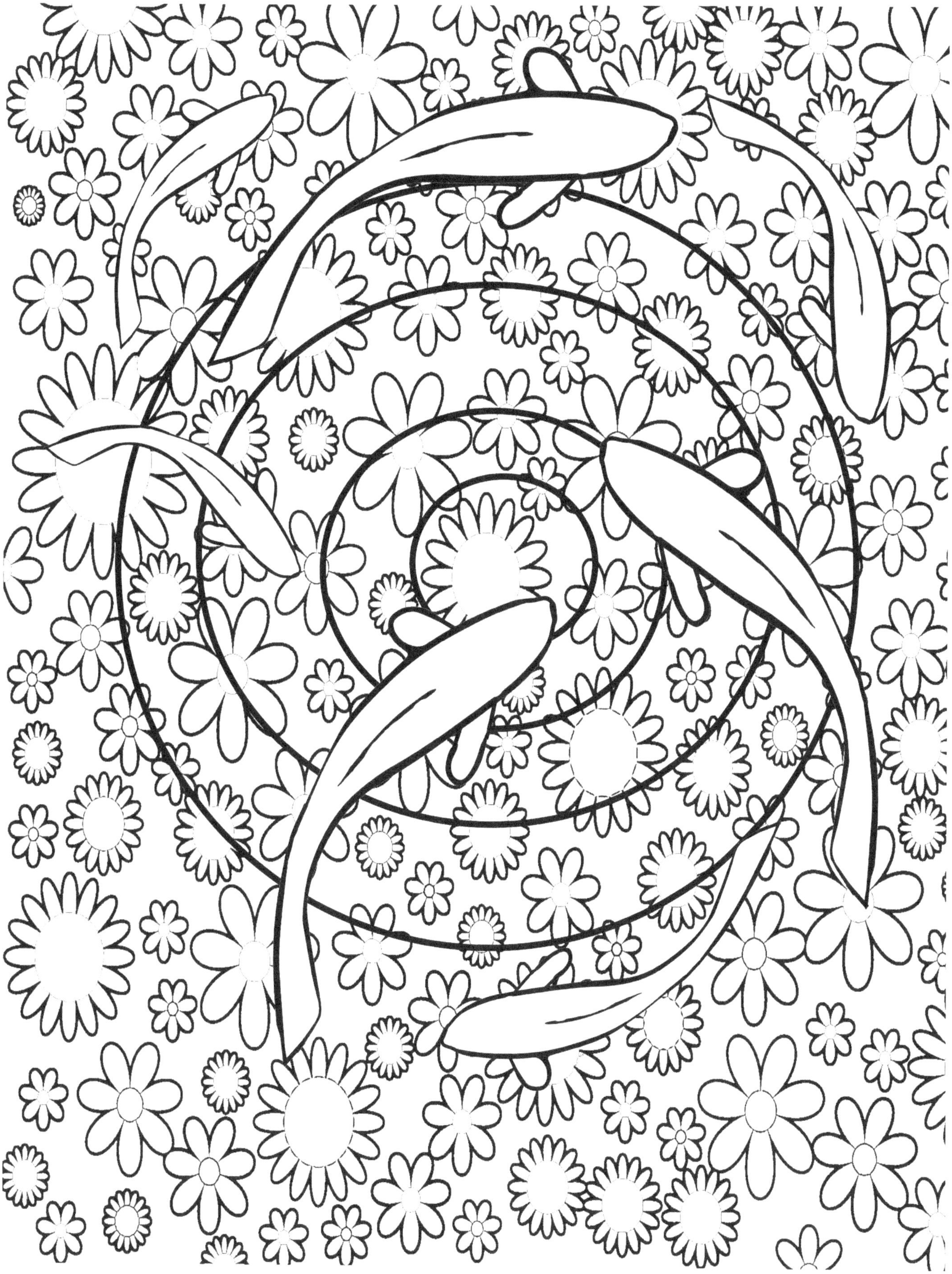

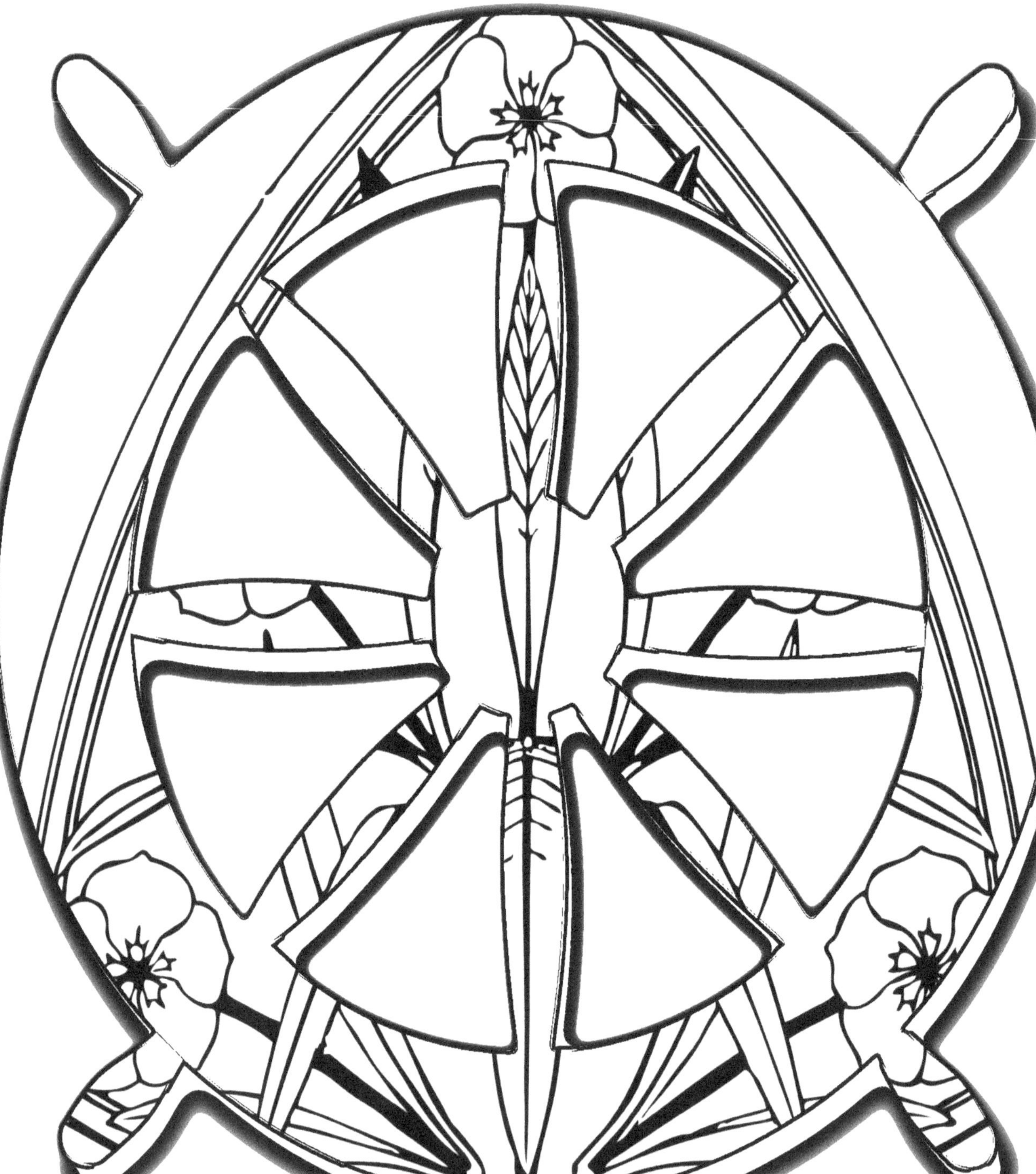

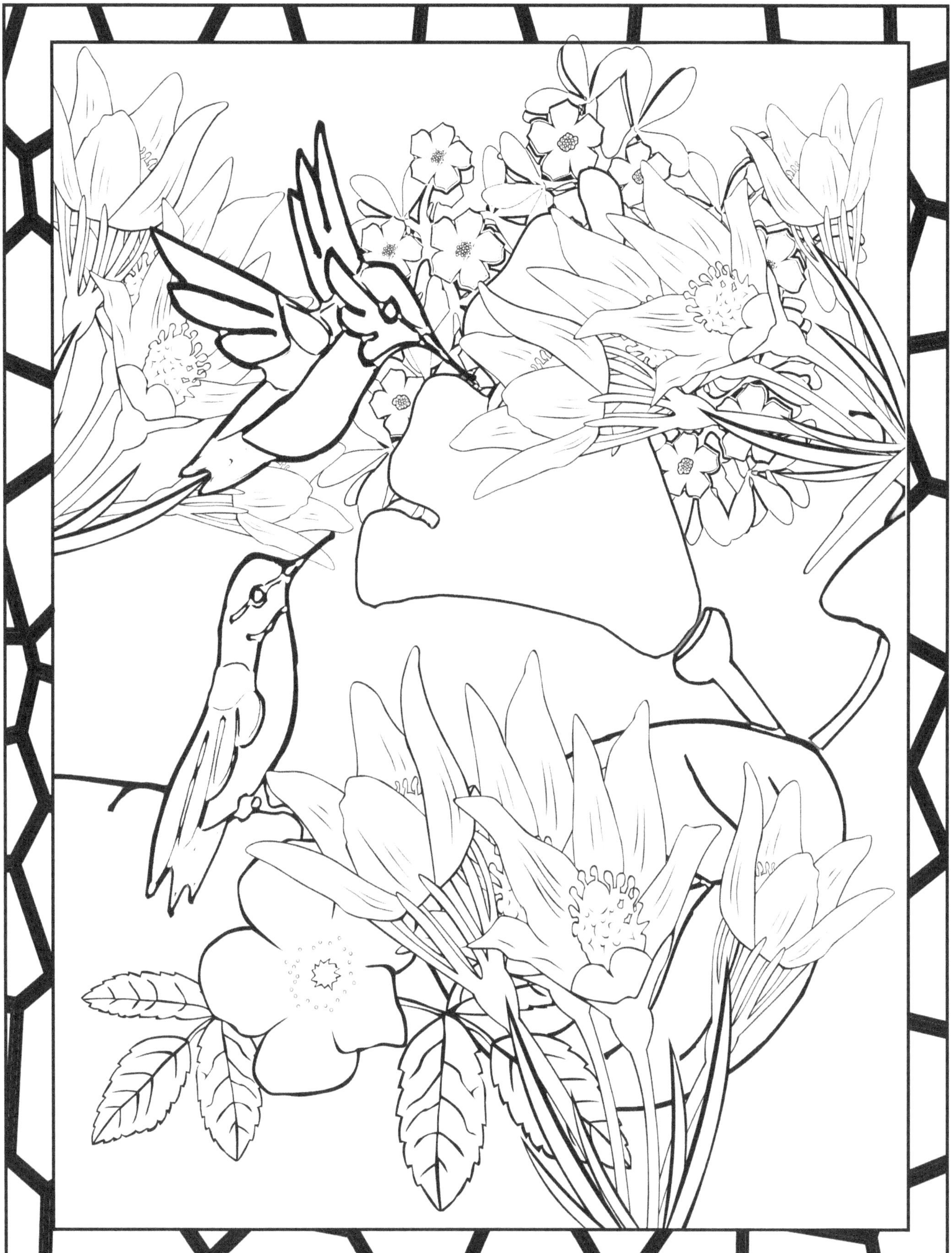

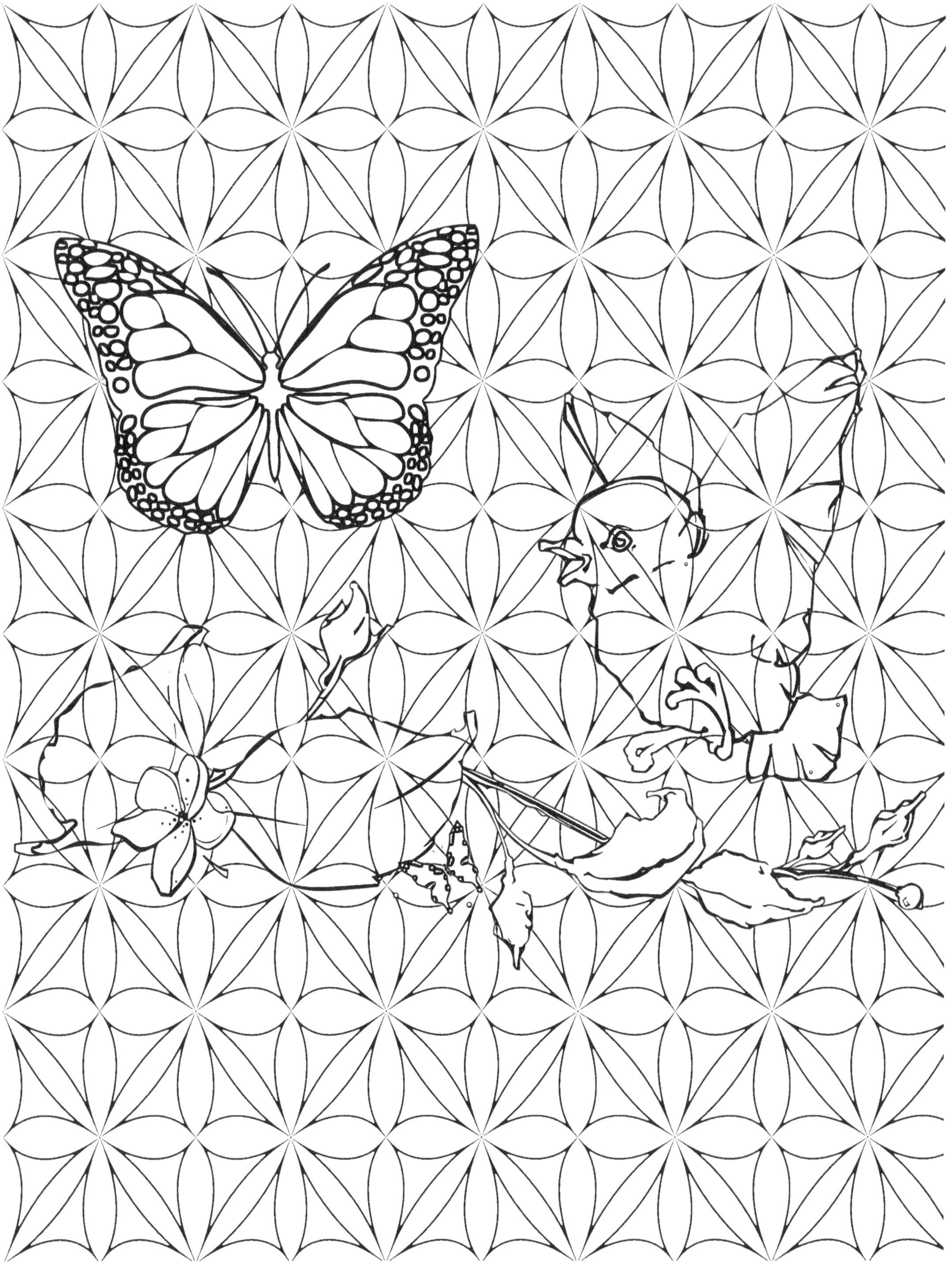

www.ingramcontent.com/pod-product-compliance
Lightning Source LLC
Chambersburg PA
CBHW080547190526
45169CB00007B/2677
9781535106290